A WORTHY MUSLIM

Quranic Tools Needed to Overcome Oppression, and Imperialism in Order to Institute Justice by Amir Makin

Post Office Box 181467
Arlington, TX 76002-1467
submissions@aicpublications.com; http://www.AICPublications.com

Copyright © 2008 by A.I.C Publications
ISBN-13: 978-0-9799464-0-0 ISBN-10: 0-9799464-0-9

Library of Congress Cataloging-in-Publication Data

Makin, Amir

A WORTHY MUSLIM: Quranic Tools Needed to Overcome Oppression, and Imperialism in Order to Institute Justice

Includes biographical references and index

ISBN-13: 978-0-9799464-0-0 (pbk.: alk. Paper)

1.Religion, Islam—United States I. Makin, Amir II. Title 2. Race & Politics Studies I. Nonfiction

Library of Congress Control Number: 2007910391

Acknowledgement. . .

To those who struggle against oppression past and present and never stopped standing in the face of intimidation. I sincerely offer thanks and prayers that your struggle produces success.

FOREWORD

The author of this dynamic publication "A Worthy Muslim" has produced a most comprehensive book. Upon my reading, I find this work most informative to many persons in their quest for better understanding and enlightenment of Islam. The author conveys a stratagem of leadership that is easily communicated.

All those seeking a greater understanding of Islam will find this publication a valuable resource that will touch the very hearts of the readers. I recommend this publication be read by everyone.

Dr. Abdul-Hakeem Mohammed Sham Sud Deen
San Diego, CA

TABLE
OF
CONTENTS

INTELLECTUAL DEVELOPMENT

Knowledge is incumbent upon everyone. According to Prophet Muhammad (PBUH), we should seek knowledge from the time we are born to the time we die. An examination of great Muslim leaders makes their commitment to learning clear. They understood that an effective leader had to be educated in religion, history, math, arts and sciences to train his community effectively for independence and growth.

Here in America, slaves were forbidden to read, and teaching them was illegal. The oppressive forces in the world understand that once an oppressed person becomes educated, he knows his destiny is not to be another man's, but to be a slave of Allah. Often the most effective leaders come from the oppressed classes. When Pharaoh abused the children of Israel, he ordered all male children slaughtered. He was afraid someone from the oppressed masses would take his power, as was prophesied.

Even though Pharaoh slew many, Allah allowed Prophet Musa or Moses (PBUH) to escape. He caused Musa to be educated, and trained in the house of Pharaoh before Allah told him he was the Prophet who would win freedom for the slaves. Growing up in the house of Pharaoh, Musa (PBUH) became the ideal choice to lead because he knew Pharaoh's tactics better than anyone else.

Growing up so, Musa's (PBUH) physical and emotional training were complete, though he was not ready for leadership until Allah spoke to him and explained his true purpose. Allah explained to him that He was the Lord of all, not Pharaoh. He told Musa that man was to serve Him and no one else. He explained that He abhors oppression, and that it should be fought.

> **And slay them wherever ye catch them, and turn them out from where they have turned you out; for tumult and oppression are worse than slaughter; but fight them not at the Sacred Mosque, unless they (first) fight you there; but if they fight you, slay them. Such is the reward of those who suppress faith.**
>
> *Qur'an*
> 2:191

Allah commissioned Musa (PBUH) with the task of leading the resistance against Pharaoh's tyrannical regime. Even though Musa (PBUH) hated the oppression, he didn't know how to address it properly until Allah explained his duty to him from a spiritual perspective. This is the reason why oppressors hate Al-Islam. They know Allah detests oppression of any sort.

Prophet Muhammad (PBUH) said that Allah always accepts the supplication of the oppressed. Slaves who become educated not only learn that slavery is not their destiny but also that Allah is on their side and will help them fight oppression! That is why slaves in America were forbidden to read and Muslims brought from Africa to America in chains were separated from Al-Islam. By raising Musa up from the tribe of the oppressed, Allah gave self-esteem, dignity, honor and freedom to a people long denied.

None of that could happen, however, until Musa (PBUH) developed intellectually to face the mission Allah gave him. All prophets needed to humble themselves in several different ways to fully exercise the concepts of which Allah revealed for their specific spiritual and human conditioning.

When Allah chose Prophet Muhammad (PBUH) as the last of the prophets and messengers, He emphasized one important idea: *proclaim.*

Proclaim! In the name of thy Lord and Cherisher Who created man from a clot of blood. Proclaim! And thy Lord is Most Bountiful. He who taught the use of the pen and taught man that which he knew not. Nay, but man doth transgress all bounds. In that he looketh upon himself as self-sufficient. Verily to thy Lord is the return of all!

Qur'an 96:1-8

Allah told him the intellectual growth he needed was not general but specific, because it would keep him safe from the Lord's punishment. He instructs all mankind that if we ignore the specific intellectual growth He wants for us we will develop grand delusions of self-sufficiency. Once these delusions become manifest, vanity, conceit, and arrogance are sure to follow. Allah instructs Prophet Muhammad (PBUH) and all mankind to learn what He wants us to proclaim, though before we can proclaim correctly, we must learn correctly. He wants us to study and learn the proper nature of everything He created in its original and proper state.

He wants us to have specific growth to ensure that we and our community develop optimally as well as correctly. The amount of exposure the leader has to different areas of knowledge determines intellectual growth. After a leader gains this exposure he must devote time to understanding what he comes to know. Once he understands, Allah leads him to apply knowledge correctly. Knowing how to apply this knowledge correctly is called wisdom.

All effective leaders commit themselves seriously to intellectual development by immersing themselves in deep study. Sheikh Uthman Dan Fodio is a prime example. Born in Gobir—part of Hausaland in West Africa, now modern Nigeria and part of the Sudan—in 1168 A.H. (December 15, 1754 C.E.) Uthman Dan Fodio was first instructed in Qur'an by his father Muhammad, a scholar in Al-Islam, as well as other relatives and several North African Islamic scholars. In the Fulani language, Fodio means *learned one*.

He was known for his uncompromising commitment to Al-Islam, superb teaching skills, kind treatment toward his students and a sincere desire to perfect his piety.

He began teaching others when he was just twenty years old and still a student himself. While other imams and scholars studied classical Islamic literature for the sake of study, he focused on implementing basic Islamic practices. He taught Al-Islam from a perspective all could relate to, no matter their condition or gender, causing the community to love and value him. As a result his community grew rapidly to over sixty households.

He spoke against corrupt Muslim rulers as much as possible and urged them to follow the Qur'an and *Sunnah* instead of their own desires. The corrupt scholars refused to listen to him and increased their unjust practices. Even though his community loved and supported him, he lived a very meager life. He owned very little property and had no servants.

Many came from far away to learn from him. Returning to their homes, they taught others what they learned, so Sheikh Uthman's influence was felt in numerous lands. Uthman's popularity began to threaten the corrupt leadership. After all, since he had good moral character, knowledge of the correct application of Al-Islam, and the people's loyalty, the corrupt leaders feared the masses would demand better leadership. In 1202 A.H. (1788 C.E.), Sultan Bawa of Gobir met with Sheikh Uthman. Originally he wanted to kill the sheikh as well as his influence but reluctantly agreed to five conditions the sheikh proposed.

First, the sheikh was allowed to call people to Al-Islam without opposition. Second, no one should be prevented from following the sheikh. Third, any man wearing a turban—the dress that distinguished Muslims then—should be treated with respect. Fourth, all those thrown in prison unjustly should be freed. Finally, the sultan should not overburden his subjects with taxes.

The agreement lasted ten years, until Sultan Nafata came into power upon Bawa's death. Nafata did not honor the agreement and imposed four new conditions of his own. First, only Sheikh Uthman—and none of his students—could teach. The intended effect was to impede the spread of Al-Islam and force those in distant lands to travel in hardship. Second, no son could be converted from his father's religion. Third, all who had become Muslims were to leave Al-Islam and return to the religion of their fathers. This made people who wanted to become and remain in a state of Al-Islam criminals. Fourth, no male could wear a turban, and no female could wear a veil.

Despite this attack on Al-Islam, the sheikh continued to teach. When Nafata's son Yunfa became sultan, he attempted unsuccessfully to assassinate the sheikh. Uthman knew the Muslims' situation would only get worse, so he decided it was time to teach Muslims the essence of fighting in order to protect their faith.

By then Yunfa had amassed an army to finally deal with the Muslims and threatened to attack the sheikh's community, forcing the Muslims to make *hijra* (migrating from an unsafe country to a safe one) to a place called Gudu. Yunfa prevented as many Muslims as he could from joining the sheikh in *hijra*. He harassed them, confiscated their property and killed as many he could. The Muslims knew it was time to unite in self defense. They chose the sheikh as their *caliph* against his will, after which he was called *Amir Al-Muminin* (The Leader of the Faithful). His first order of business was to exhort Muslims to defend themselves and their right to worship Allah.

The Muslims captured two towns, and the sheikh appointed a treasurer to distribute the spoils of war according to the Qur'an and *Sunnah*. After the victorious battle, Sheikh Uthman's son Muhammad Bello went to Muslim leaders in different provinces with a letter from the sheikh inviting them to make *ba'ya* (a pledge of allegiance and unity of leadership) to him and to unite with other Muslims against the enemies of Al-

Islam, as Qu'ran and *Sunnah* require.

The leaders accepted, and they all fought united until 1223 A.H. when Sultan Yunfa was killed and his forces defeated. After appointing *amirs* (caliph appointed leaders who carry out specific duties in target locations) in different provinces to protect Muslim interests, Sheikh Uthman designed a flag to signify the caliphate's unity. After the long struggle, he finally returned to teaching and writing.

To ensure Muslims would recognize potential future catastrophes, he regularly taught against oppression and the abuse of power. In 1230 A.H. (1815 C.E.) he moved to Sokoto, where his son established a town. Sheikh Uthman died there two years later at the age of sixty-three.

The establishment of the Sokoto caliphate was a very important event in the Muslim community throughout the world, because African Muslims suffered the same type of oppression as did the Prophet Muhammad (PBUH) and his followers in their time. Because he studied and practiced Al-Islam, however, Sheikh Uthman knew that if he reacted as Muhammad (PBUH) did, he could also triumph similarly.

The sheikh's commitment to study distinguished him from all other teachers. His intellectual level let him adopt methods of teaching Al-Islam that addressed everyone's individual condition.

He was able to study and teach concurrently. He did not let what he did not know prevent him from achieving his goal. He undertook intellectual training early in his life and made of intellectual development a habitual necessity. Had he not committed to learning, the people would have had no leader to protect them in the practice of Al-Islam. Had he not studied intensely, he could not have taught people effectively. Had he been unable to teach the people, he could not have gotten to know them. Had he not known the people, he could not have led them.

Prophet Muhammad (PBUH) said, "Surely, Allah will send for this *ummah* (community) at the advent of every one hundred years a person (or persons) who will revive its religion for it."

That is the definition of a *mujadid* which Sheikh Uthman Dan Fodio fit. His commitment to intellectual development is still felt in modern Nigeria, as Islamic scholars still teach using his methods. When a leader develops his intellect, he breaks the psychological chains society seeks to impose. Once the chains come off, nothing but the will of Allah can stop him from achieving excellence.

> **And if all the trees in the
> earth were pens, and the sea, with
> seven more seas to help it, (were
> ink), the words of Allah could not**

be exhausted! Lo! Allah is Mighty,
Wise.

Qur'an 31:27

As the knowledge of Allah cannot be exhausted, neither can the process of intellectual development. Allah wants such excellence for us as caliphs, as leaders of ourselves, our families and our communities. To prevent us from realizing that, unjust societies refuse to recognize the intelligent among the oppressed. They hope to make you live for *their* acclaim, *their* prestige and *their* rewards. *They* mean to define the standard you aspire to. A Muslim leader with proper insight of his mission lives for the rewards of Allah and defines excellence by the standard of Qur'an and *Sunnah*. A leader with an outlook like Uthman Dan Fodio's will always overcome oppression and succeed: **"Ye shall surely travel from stage to stage"** (*Qur'an* 84:19*)*.

To prevent the masses from realizing their purpose for existence, the media intentionally distorts Al-Islam. To counter that, we must develop a constant state of awareness that leads to an equal state of consciousness. Awareness means using the senses of perception Allah has blessed us with to develop a complete understanding of the environment all around us. That requires intense study, commitment to learning and understanding, as well as an undying passion for adjusting personally to promote learning in your family. To do that, one must first understand how the environment affects him, for better for worse.

Some key event in a person's life often causes him to begin to examine matters. For some, it takes the loss of wealth, for others perhaps the loss of a loved one. Sadly, far too many must suffer the consequences of living a wrongful life to come to fruition. Regardless of the circumstances, a person must examine his life to grow, prosper and excel, else he cannot optimize his full potential.

People who cannot realize their full potential can never help others with theirs.

Unplanned things happen perhaps to shock people stuck in a negative state into a more positive state. What if such a key event occurs early in life? If that happens, the person has a jumpstart on optimizing his entire life and improving the life of his family and community! Because the examination requires intense study, a person must study what is correct. Though a child may study for hours, if he believes two plus two equals five, he must learn anew. That is why when Muhammad (PBUH) was told he was the last Messenger of Allah he was also told to proclaim or recite, not in general but a set of specifics.

Allah told him to proclaim in the name of His Lord, so what he understood about his environment would be seen the way Allah intended. That established both his environmental awareness and his direction. Al-Islam must be taken with both the Qur'an and the patterns and examples of the prophets and messengers. The Qur'an provides this awareness, while the life patterns and examples of the prophets and messengers show the method of execution, known as *active* consciousness.

For example, when someone inside his home hears drops falling on the window pane, he looks outside and sees rain. To know how intense the rain is, he sticks his hand through the window and understands that the environment is not only wet but also that prolonged exposure could produce anything from a cold to pneumonia. He then begins to consider options to protect himself from either likelihood. He says either "I'm going to stay inside until this passes" or "I'm going to put on a raincoat." Awareness leads people to take proper actions or go to the next logical step, which is active consciousness. Active consciousness without awareness is impossible.

Awareness without consciousness is a crime. When a person has awareness without consciousness, he either has a passive mindset or has been spiritually, psychologically and ideologically conditioned to accept a harmful environment as normal, thus impeding his developmental awareness. Such a person will not fully understand his condition, but because he accepts it as normal may even attack others with environmental awareness and active consciousness because he views them as abnormal. Awareness without any consciousness is a state of oppression that advances addiction, genocide, fratricide and other social ills that manifest around the world. The status of the disenfranchised Black community results from a calculated effort to destroy active consciousness and minimize awareness. The origins of this tactic can also be explained in the Qur'an.

The *Shaytan* (Satan) admitted as much to Allah by saying: **"I will surely make wrong fair seeming to them (mankind) and I will mislead them all except among them, Your chosen servants"** (*Qur'an* 15:39-40).

The reason Prophet Muhammad (PBUH) succeeded is that he constantly advocated the correct environmental awareness. Consequently, he was able to prepare and strategize against the tactics of his enemies through active consciousness. As a result Allah blessed his efforts, which are still felt today.

Another major problem arises with others who have environmental awareness but feel a sense of reward for ignoring it. Some Muslim leaders may promote the building of *masjids* (places of prayer), community learning centers and businesses in one neighborhood but oppose the same things in another. They know the establishment of such institutions enables communities to take charge of their educational, social, economic and political directions, yet they don't advance the same ideas elsewhere because they want the benefits of independence for themselves alone.

An important step in developing leadership is mastery of the self, setting and controlling one's own agenda, which comes only when a person is fully aware of his own value and self worth. *All* forms of oppression seek to prevent that from occurring. Unfortunately, a conditioned lack of awareness to human victimization has led some non-Muslims and many Muslims to victimize others. As a result, many who wrongly turn to such people for validation are driven deeper and deeper into oppression.

Another reason Allah said, "Proclaim in the name of thy Lord who created you," was to instill the understanding that His validation and His alone should matter. Prophet Muhammad (PBUH), in spite of being told to proclaim, could neither read nor write. Many societies call a person like this lazy, stupid or dumb and stigmatize them as unable to produce anything positive that requires cognitive thought. Yet Prophet Muhammad (PBUH) did not seek validation of his humanity and self worth from the society. He turned directly to Allah, and Allah revealed to him what he should proclaim and eventually pass on to mankind. Many Muslims and non-Muslims who suffer from the cancer of racism must be reminded of this when they dismiss certain people they despise as worthless. People must begin to go back to the historical origins of all to understand how they must keep these original concepts safe from perversion.

I use the term *Al-Islam* instead of *Islam* for two reasons. First, Al-Islam means *the Islam* and refers to the correct environmental awareness Allah reveals in the Qur'an and the consciousness the prophets exemplified as the only standard for Muslims. The second reason is that some ignorantly define Islam by any and everything that comes from a so-called Muslim country, not realizing that some if not most matters in such countries have nothing to do with Al-Islam. The mistaken perception comes when such countries overemphasize ethnic identity instead of the correct understanding and awareness of Allah which should under gird ethnic, tribal and religious cultures.

I will focus primarily on areas that have known oppression at its worst because those areas need Al-Islam most and have been grossly underserved by those who profit from their oppression. I will identify qualities essential to overcoming oppression, qualities I feel have not been identified properly in people in geographical areas hardest hit by oppression—ghettos, barrios, trailer parks and jails. Throughout this book, you will notice that I note PBUH which means *Peace be upon him* after the names of the prophets and messengers. That is because Allah says:

> **Say ye: "We believe in Allah,**
> **and the revelation given to us, and**
> **to Abraham, Isma'il, Isaac, Jacob,**
> **and the Tribes, and that given to**
> **Moses and Jesus, and that given to**

(all) prophets from their Lord: We make no difference between one and another of them: And we bow to Allah (in Islam)."

Qur'an 2:136

No prophet is more important than another. They all served their Lord faithfully and with due diligence. Each built upon the mission of his predecessor. Since they all taught the same message and worshipped the same Creator, they deserve to be respected the same.

All too often people in power write the oppressed off as worthless because they have no significant economic or political power. Al-Islam addresses oppression and people who feel trapped by it. Al-Islam says no one is worthless unless he chooses a worthless life. Al-Islam established those principles long before there was a Constitution or a Declaration of Independence.

Al-Islam would not call anyone three-fifths of a person, as the original U.S. Constitution categorized Black people. Al-Islam teaches that socioeconomic problems and those who profit from them must not go unchallenged. Hence Al-Islam is for people, Muslim or non-Muslim, who have been abandoned or neglected, for those who can't fight for themselves. It is for the poor, the physically challenged, the wrongly imprisoned (either physically or spiritually). It is for those who are too light skinned or too dark skinned. It is for those who have been told, "You're nothing." Al-Islam rejects that, and so should you.

This book seeks to analyze the active consciousness of the prophets and messengers and explain how to find the sense of self worth from within that Allah intends for all. These qualities will be examined in the actions and patterns of the prophets and messengers using Qur'anic examples and language. Some verses will appear more than once to show the great diversity of their correct applications. *A Worthy Muslim* is about optimizing the full potential of mankind and achieving the true leadership which must be attained in stages for excellence.

STAGES
OF
LEADERSHIP

Prophet Muhammad (PBUH) said that children come into this world natural Muslims, but their parents either enforce a proper Islamic environment or change it and take children away from their natural Muslim nature. The Prophet (PBUH) meant that children have no control over their bodies. They can neither protect nor provide for themselves. Their bodies and everything around them submits entirely to the will of Allah, which makes them submissive consciously and subconsciously to Allah. Their souls have not yet been exposed to what is wrong, so their natural inclination is for the good. Yet, children must develop and grow.

According to Prophet Muhammad (PBUH), humans are to be nurtured in three mental stages. First, when a child enters the world as a baby, it is considered a king. At that stage, parents shower their children with love, affection and adoration. They spoil them and give them anything they desire, so children learn that their parents are the first who love them. They in turn feel, love, honor, obedience and respect for their parents.

A second stage begins when children turn seven. They become indentured servants to their parents. In addition to spiritual obligations, they undertake easy levels of responsibility, such as doing chores around the house. They have assignments in school they must complete. They realize that the world will not spoil them as their parents did and learn they must earn a living and struggle at it. During this stage they understand they must be prepared to face the consequences of not fulfilling their duties, crucial to understanding how to survive.

Parents explain to their children their purpose for being created and the mission they must fulfill. They urge children to embrace the good and forbid the bad, regardless of what the world says. Children learn that true objectives and morality come from Allah, His Messenger (PBUH) and no one else. Every parent's duty is to teach that mission; every child's duty is to receive it to prepare for the final mental stage: full responsibility.

At that stage, children become adults, fully equipped with knowledge of their mission and purpose and the tools needed for success. They are charged to build upon the knowledge their parents provided in the second stage and to continue learning on their own, to act on their newfound intelligence and to grow in discipline. They will have challenges to their growth that will first come from within themselves such as their wants and passions. People must exercise control of their base desires and corrupt inclinations.

Adults must be ready to teach what they have learned to those closest to them, their families. Those they teach should carry on the mission passed down to them, to be not just adults but leaders. Only those who understand that can ever gain true leadership. That is the natural state Allah created mankind in, and that is our destiny.

When an automobile manufacturer builds a car, all the parts needed to make up the engine are assembled onto a block. Then comes the outer shell, things like tires, doors, axles, transmission, hood and trunk are over the block. Once it's painted, it may finally be called a car.

True leaders must be nurtured the same way. From birth they are trained to take different parts of development and apply them. They gain additional knowledge, responsibility, and discipline, until one day they glisten with the finishing paint of real leadership. True leaders are not born but manufactured.

This book is for those ready to accept the responsibility of true leadership and attain the potential within themselves, for those who will never stop learning, never stop teaching. It is for those who put the commands of Allah first and foremost in their lives and are ready to fear Allah and no one else. It is for those who will stand up for justice in good and bad times, those who realize Al-Islam is not a religion but an all encompassing way of life. It is for those who understand their reward, better than anything in this life, will come from Allah. That is the essence of the Islamic movement, the heart of Muslim activism. In this sense the role of leader is defined; in this way leaders are manufactured. When this role is realized, the leader can train others in understanding their natural state of existence.

THE NATURE OF MAN

I have only created Jinns and men,
that they may serve Me.

Qur'an 51:56

According to the verse, Allah created mankind to worship Him alone. Once we know our purpose is to worship Him, the next question is, "How do we worship Him?" Allah bestowed upon man the right of guarding the earth and using all the blessings He put here. Mankind is to use those blessings to support all that is good and oppose what is wrong.

Verily We have created man into toil and struggle. Thinketh he, that none hath power over him? He may say (boastfully); Wealth have I squandered in abundance! Thinketh he that none beholdeth him? Have We not made for him a pair of eyes? And a tongue, and a pair of lips? And shown him the two highways? But he hath made no haste on the path that is steep. And what will explain to thee the path that is steep? (It is:) freeing the bondman; Or the giving of food in a day of privation to the orphan with claims of relationship, or to the indigent (down) in the dust. Then will he be of those who believe, and enjoin patience, (constancy, and self-restraint), and

> enjoin deeds of kindness and com-
> passion. Such are the Companions
> of the Right Hand.
>
> *Qur'an* 90:4-18

Here Allah means to teach us that by adhering to His knowledge, we know what to undertake and what to avoid. By this application, we may discern the correct position to lead.

Allah intended us to struggle against the bad inclinations that plague everyone. To overcome them, we need a proper understanding of why we were created, the direction our Creator has marked out for us, the tools for victory he has given us.

The struggle strengthens us with good *iman* (faith) and shows us how strong we are. It also helps Allah determine if we are worthy of paradise. By rising above evil suggestions, leaders establish good moral character, a sense of responsibility and discipline and insure they will obey Allah alone. That frees them from slavery, to men or to vice. Leaders recognize that the enemies of justice use those tools to prevent people from achieving ultimate success.

The American government lets drugs and alcohol run rampant in the ghettos. Addictions cause women to prostitute themselves, increase the spread of AIDS and divert money that could be used for building *masjids*, schools, businesses and community development centers from the people who need them most. That contributes to the systematic destruction of a people, which amounts to genocide.

Imagine the effect when someone comes into the knowledge of proper leadership. He is not inclined to the vices a society intent on destroying him puts in his way. He can instill that knowledge in his family, his neighbor's family and another family. He has created a community—productive, independent and capable of resisting corruption from without and within.

The community can then develop schools, hospitals, grocery stores and other businesses that produce economic, political and social independence. That is the true essence of freedom all oppressed people seek, the true essence of freedom Allah created mankind for. Once leaders recognize true freedom, they become uncompromising in their faith. They fear their Lord like no other and prefer death to living any other way. True leaders know they are responsible to understand the correct application of knowledge for all in their charge. They know when they make mistakes, as they are bound to do, they must account to Allah for them.

Therefore a leader's *taqwa* (fear of Allah) should be greater than anyone else's. Because of that, leaders struggle to maintain a perpetual state of obedience and reverence for their Lord. That is why Prophet Muhammad (PBUH) said "the best one to lead is he who doesn't want leadership." Someone once asked the second caliph named Umar if he would appoint his successor or let the people do it. He replied that he would let the people resolve the matter rather than make the appointment himself.

He also said that people are of two kinds: those keen to take the position of caliph and those afraid of such responsibility for fear of doing wrong. Leaders with the proper understanding of leadership prefer to be free from responsibility because they understand that Allah will hold them accountable for their actions and the actions of those in their charge whose behavior is a direct result of their leadership.

Athletes who want to excel push their bodies to the limit by undertaking new pressures continuously. They eat a nutritious diet and adopt a demanding fitness plan. All the while they avoid bad foods, bad drinks and all types of laziness. They don't care if they act alone because they know they are on the right track. They don't care what others think of them because they hope for the maximum reward and, as a result, become the best. The competition is no match. They achieve success and enjoy the fruits of their labors. That is the attitude of Muslim leaders. They must first understand why they are alive and know that their ultimate objective is paradise, then use all they have to gain that reward.

The nutrition for the soul is the Book of Allah and His Messenger's (PBUH) application of it. Leaders' spiritual muscles become strong by resisting the whispers of the *Shaytan* and his agents and trusting in Allah with patience and constancy. Their intellectual muscles become powerful as they immerse themselves in a never-ending search for knowledge. Their emotional state improves as they surround themselves with others on the same path.

They use the gifts Allah gives—sight, touch, hearing, taste and smell—to ensure they remain conscious of their surroundings and steady on the right path. They use the gift of speech to teach their families, their community, and bear witness for themselves to those around them. Leaders push themselves to the limit by trying to perfect their worship constantly. Such are the Companions of The Right Hand.

Prophet Muhammad (PBUH) said that no caliph is appointed without two groups of advisors. One advises him to do good, and the other advises him to do evil. Only those whom Allah protects can rise above that.

That is the intended position of Muslim leaders. Any who goes against that corrupts his own soul.

Verily Man is in loss. Except such as have Faith, and do righteous deeds, and (join together) in the mutual teaching of Truth, and of Patience and Constancy.

*Qur'an:*103

Once a person realizes this, he must change his diet. He must now adopt a perpetual state of spiritual nourishment. Following are five foods consisting of this spiritual meal.

THE
SPIRITUAL
DIET

Everyone has debts; some, debts on top of debts. Imagine the gas or water company charging for services but not collecting from you because you're a friend of the CEO. Imagine those same companies providing you free service because you sit on the board of directors. The *salat* (prayer) of the Muslim works that way. It helps cultivate good relations between Allah and His servant. The better the relation, the closer the servant becomes to his Lord.

Prophet Muhammad (PBUH) asked if someone would be dirty if he bathed in a clean stream five times a day. The response was negative. That is another benefit *salat* provides for the soul. Many people do not understand the Muslim *salat* because their hearts and minds have not been opened to grasp its complete significance. Yet it is one of the most beneficial tools in the leader's arsenal. It is one part of real faith.

True faith must be evident in three ways. First, our hearts must open to understand our true reason for being. Allah judges all actions by intent, so what lives in the heart bears witness to Allah. Then we must declare our faith through speech, because that bears witness to us ourselves. Finally we must implement faith through acts and deeds of worship that complement what is in our hearts and mouths. That creates three-part harmony among heart, tongue and actions. This is the meaning of righteousness. The right intent and the right words must produce the right deeds that are performed in order to worship and thus fulfill mankind's true reason for existence.

These acts of worship must be identical to the way Prophet Muhammad (PBUH) and all other prophets and messengers before him worshipped.

> **Ye have indeed in the Messenger of Allah a beautiful pattern for any one whose hope is in Allah and the Final Day, and who engages much in the Praise of Allah.**
>
> *Qur'an* 33:21

Believers who engage in *salat* mean to please Allah and gain His favor. They confirm their faith in their Lord through reciting the Lord's Word in the Qur'an. They then extend their faith through physical movements.

We bend and bow, prostrating the body on the ground in humility before the Lord. We harmonize and fulfill all three conditions of true faith through one act of prayer. At that moment faith is perfected, and Allah loves us for it. We become closer and dearer to Allah than anyone else.

If we walk toward Allah, He runs toward us. Consequentially, Allah has said that if someone declares war on His pious servant, He declares war on the aggressor. The key word is pious, which means remaining obedient to the commands of Allah.

Believers don't pray merely because they have been ordered to; they pray for strength from Allah, for wisdom, for forgiveness of sins, both intentional and unintentional. Believers make *salat* to find peace of mind and contentment, to succeed in this life and the next.

When believers gain Allah's favor through prayer, Allah forgives their sins and gives them strength to refrain from sin. The same way the gas and water company would forgo the debt, there exists the possibility that Allah will restrain the punishment believers deserve as long as they seek forgiveness and guidance through *salat*. Believers understand the attention they pay to remembering Allah is directly related to the conditions of their lives.

Many rich and powerful people in the world have so much money they could not spend it in a lifetime. They have all the attention they want. They devote all their time and energy to getting wealth or influence, and that passion consumes them. Yet many become alcoholics, drug abusers, gambling addicts or just plain miserable.

> **But whosoever turns away from My Message verily for him is a life narrowed down and We shall raise him up blind on the Day of**

Judgment.

Qur'an 20:124

Further, Allah says that if we all commit ourselves to His worship, He fills our hearts with contentment and removes poverty; if not He fills our hearts
with nothing but the world's concerns and leaves us in
poverty. Allah does not deprive us merely of money but
of the inner peace and solace we need to survive. Without *salat*, the soul cannot draw its full strength. That is
why many cannot understand this requirement upon
Muslims.

The first two items on the menu of spiritual
food are bearing witness that Allah alone is Lord, and
establishing *salat*. The third piece is fasting.

> **Ramadan is the (month) in
> which was sent down the Qur'an,
> as a guide to mankind, also clear
> (Signs) for guidance and judgment
> (Between right and wrong). So
> every one of you who is present (at
> his home) during that month
> should spend it in fasting, but if
> any one is ill, or on a journey, the
> prescribed period (Should be made
> up) by days later.**

Qur'an 2:178

Prophet Muhammad (PBUH) said the sins of

anyone who fasts the month of Ramadan out of sincere faith to attain Allah's rewards are forgiven their past sins. He also emphasized that when Ramadan starts, the gates of Heaven are opened, the gates of Hell are closed and the devils are chained. In addition to that, he stressed two pleasures for people who fast, one received when breaking the fast, the other when meeting our Lord and achieving the full reward for fasting. Fasting is a shield as well as a protection from the fires of Hell and sin.

Fasting in the month of Ramadan provides those benefits and more. Fasting helps leaders become self-controlled, as it checks the desire for wrong things. It also gives people empathy for those with far less than we. That empathy makes us notice those we come in contact with and increases our compassion. As compassion increases, the potential for tyranny diminishes. All that sets leaders in motion to give more out of compassion and help others improve their condition. That prepares us for the fourth item on the spiritual diet: *zakat* or charity.

Zakat is an amount those who can afford, give annually from their total wealth. After they pay their debts, take care of themselves and their families, they pay 2.5% of what remains of their wealth as *zakat,* which provides not only for the indigent, the sick, and people in hardship but also stimulates the entire society economically. Prophet Muhammad (PBUH) taught that *zakat* is for the following people only: those fighting in the way of Allah, those whose only job is to collect *zakat* from the people, those who have suffered financial loss at the hands of debtors, those who buy it with their own money, and those with poor neighbors who receive *zakat* and give it to others in need.

> **Zakat expenditures are only for the poor, and for the needy and for those employed to collect [the zakat], and for bringing hearts together, and for freeing captives [slaves], and for those in debt and for the cause of Allah and for the traveler, an obligation imposed by Allah. And Allah is Knowing and Wise.**
>
> *Qur'an* 9:60

> **Take [O Muhammad] from their wealth a charity by which you purify them and cause them increase, and invoke [Allah's Blessings] upon them. Indeed your invocations are reassurance for them. And Allah is Hearing and Knowing.**
>
> *Qur'an* 9:103

Zakat is an investment. After we perform *zakat* Allah increases the provisions of those who give it. It trains us not to look to those above us but at those in worse conditions than ours. That increases our gratitude for all the blessings the Lord sends. The more gratitude we show to Allah, the more He assists us in our daily struggles. Once leaders render *zakat*, people realize they care as much for their followers' condition as for their own. They see their leaders as neither selfish nor miserly but truly compassionate. They realize their society and government will support them, which encourages them to support their leaders.

In any oppressive society, freedom fighters usually emerge from the indigent. Resistance to oppression hardly ever comes from the wealthy elite, because resistance threatens its position of power. The Black Liberation Movement in America culminated in the 1960s Black Power Movement which started in the ghetto. The Deacons for Defense started in the poorest areas of Louisiana, not only because the Ku Klux Klan brutally killed Blacks but also because the federal government did nothing to prevent these forms of terrorism.

The 1950s Mau Mau Rebellion in Kenya started because the British occupied Kenya illegally and refused to recognize the human rights of the Kenyan people. Nat Turner's slave rebellion started because racist Whites treated Blacks worse than animals. Resistance by indigent people usually starts with some form of civil disobedience—strikes or walk outs—to protest unfair wage practices, unjust treatment by the legal system or inaccessibility to opportunities everyone else enjoys.

If civil disobedience does not work, the oppressed realize the only thing power respects is power and rush to gain power regardless of the means, including full-scale war with high casualties. If there is no war, the divide based on race and class, the line between the haves and the have nots, becomes permanent.

This causes the oppression to continue only in a different form. Once divided, hypocrisy becomes the norm of society and there remains no just place to live. *Zakat* addresses much of the problem by increasing mutual cooperation and reducing the climate of anarchy, tribalism and nationalism. In a proper economic system of Al-Islam (which does not exist today), the poor are not disregarded because they have the right to be provided for. Not only is that in the best interest of society, it is Allah's commandment.

The last spiritual menu item is *hajj* or pilgrimage, a journey required of all Muslims at least once in their lifetime. The journey leads to the Ka'bah in Mecca, the first place of worship Prophet Ibrahim or Abraham (PBUH) and his son Prophet Ismail or Ishmael (PBUH) built.

Indeed the first House of worship established for mankind was that at Mecca – blessed and a guidance for the worlds. In it are clear signs such as the standing place of Ibrahim. And whoever enters it shall be safe. And due to Allah

> **from the people is a pilgrimage to the House – for whoever is able to find thereto a way. But whoever disbelieves – then indeed, Allah is free from need of the worlds.**
>
> *Qu'ran* 3:96-97

In addition to fulfilling Allah's command, performing *hajj* yields other benefits. Prophet Muhammad (PBUH) said that anyone who performs *hajj* for Allah's pleasure and avoids all lewdness and sins will return after *hajj* free from sin like a newborn baby. Further, the Ka'bah (the House of Allah) is the pillar of Al-Islam, and Allah spiritually protects anyone who travels there for *hajj*.

If the one performing *hajj* dies during the trip he gains paradise; those who return home safely are rewarded for the trip. The term *house,* recall, does not mean Muslims think Allah *lives* there, but it is the first place Ibrahim (PBUH) and his son Ismail (PBUH) built under Allah's divine instruction expressly for the purpose of worshipping Allah. The formation of the Ka'bah involves the story of the struggle of Ibrahim (PBUH), his wife Hajjar or Hagar and their son Ismail (PBUH). When Muslims perform *hajj*, we relive that history and perform the same acts those righteous servants performed. That means that part of the *hajj* rituals are performed to revere a woman's struggle, and Allah expects Muslims to consider the plight of women carefully. Additionally, Muslims who make the journey often gain their own personal enlightenment.

El Hajj Malik El Shabazz, better known as Malcolm X, made *hajj*, and it completely transformed his thinking. He grew up in a country defined by racial superiority for White people, and he reacted by hating them. Once he made *hajj*, he then saw himself as a complete member of Allah's creation with the same talents as anyone else. *Hajj* let Malik Shabazz redefine his self image in accordance with the will and plan of Allah. He saw people of many colors and races all in the same place to please their Lord. He realized that Allah intended to accentuate and complement everyone by making each different.

Hajj is not just a trip but a journey believers make to feel closer to their Lord than anywhere else in the world, a physical migration that gives believers an opportunity to see the power of the unity belief in Allah generates. It is emotionally uplifting because it promotes brotherhood based on piety and nothing else: **"For them there will be the double reward for what they did, and they will be in the upper chambers of paradise, safe and secure"** (*Qur'an* 34:37).

Hajj forces believers to set their spiritual focus on the right track, to realize that their ultimate return is to Allah. Thus believers renew their faith and commitment to strive for Allah. *Hajj* fortifies leaders for the fight against injustice. Visiting the only structure built by Divine Instruction, leaders feel closer to all Allah's prophets because they know they are walking the same route as those great servants of Allah before them. Leaders become conscious that the only way to succeed is to follow the example of the prophets who have gained Allah's favor.

El Hajj Malik El Shabazz returned to America able to see the racial problem for what it really was: man's rejection of the commandments of Allah.

> **O mankind, indeed We have created you from male and female and made you nations and tribes that you may know one another. Indeed the most noble of you in the sight of Allah is the most righteous of you. Indeed Allah is Knowing and Acquainted.**
>
> *Qur'an* 49:13

That is why he declared the racial superiority of Blacks he preached before was just as wrong as the racial superiority Whites taught. He declared that Al-Islam was the only true hope America had to prevent its own suicide. By doing so, he was urging the soul of the country to seek its own redemption beginning with its supplication.

VALUE
OF
THE
DUA

In a war there are many weapons that can be used in defense of one's position. Many countries use guns, and bombs. Yet, Muslims have one additional weapon that no one else possesses.

> **And your Lord said, Invoke Me, and I will respond to your (invocation). Verily those who scorn My worship they will surely enter Hell in humiliation!**
>
> *Qur'an* 40:60

That invocation is called a *dua* in Arabic, and all the prophets used them. Muhammad (PBUH) said that all the prophets had special *duas* they routinely used in their daily quests. Even though the *dua* is essential to anyone struggling against injustice, it works only if the supplicant meets certain criteria explained here. Sulayman, also known as Solomon (PBUH) met those criteria.

> **And Solomon inherited (the knowledge of) David. He said: O mankind! We have been taught the language of birds, and on us have been bestowed all things. This, verily, is an evident grace (from Allah).**
>
> *Qur'an* 27:16

The Qur'an explains that Sulayman (PBUH) had knowledge, wisdom and the kingdom of his father,

Prophet Daud or David (PBUH). He could communicate with birds and animals alike. He had also a copper mine, and Allah ordered him to mine the earth and extract minerals to manufacture tools and weapons. He had many horses at a time when horses were as essential as automobiles are today. One day as he admired his horses' the beauty and stature, the time for the middle prayer (Asr) came and went. When he realized he missed the prayer he said, **"Truly do I love the love of good with a view to the glory of my Lord"** (*Qur'an* 38:32). He found admiring his gifts more important than worshipping Allah. He paid a heavy price to learn the error of his ways. Allah took away his kingdom.

> **And We did try Solomon: We placed on his throne a body without life (a Jasadan – a devil, that was placed on his throne in his place so he lost his kingdom); but he (Sulayman) did turn to Allah with obedience and repentance.**
>
> *Qur'an* 38:34

Sulayman (PBUH) made a crucial mistake many struggling against oppression still make. He let the things we admire most distract him from his mission to worship the way Allah wanted. Yet he took action, made amends and got another opportunity. When Sulayman (PBUH) recognized his error, he said, **"O my Lord! Forgive me and grant me a kingdom which suits** none another after me: for Thou art the Grantor of **Bounties (without measure)**" (*Qur'an* 38:35). That was the *dua* unique to **his** prophethood. Allah then restored his kingdom and granted him power unlike any other.

> **Then We subjected the Wind to his power to flow gently to his order whithersoever he willed. As also the evil ones (jinns) including every kind of builder and diver. As also others bound together in fetters. Such are Our Bounties: whether thou bestow them (on others) or withhold them no account will be asked. And he enjoyed indeed a Near Approach to Us and a beautiful place of (final) Return.**
>
> *Qur'an* 38:36-40

All that in addition to his previous power, wealth and stature! The question is, why would Sulayman (PBUH) receive more power than he had before after making the mistake that cost him his power in the first place? The answer can be given in stages.

First, note that many prophets made mistakes. A mistake is unlike a sin in that a sin is something we do knowing well and completely understanding that Allah forbids it. We intentionally disregard the law to insult Allah. None of the prophets and messengers did this.

Prophets were sinless, yet made mistakes as do all humans. However they never let their mistakes stop them from learning and overcoming.

People fighting injustice must remember the same. All too often people hold others to unreasonably high standards that leave no room for error. Mistakes are a *necessary* fact of life. Allah said that if some group of people never committed sins, He would wipe them out and create people who sin to force them to seek forgiveness. We cannot attain wisdom without learning from past mistakes. Wisdom is the correct application of knowledge and understanding in any situation. Sulayman (PBUH) learned from his experience and proved himself able to handle additional responsibility. In so doing, he rose above one obstacle to be tested with another.

Wealth can be as great a trial as poverty. Poor people ordinarily ask for greater riches. The petitions of the rich are usually different. Both ask according to their material needs or desires, but the *dua* of the Muslim is an extension of his faith. The Muslims' *dua* accords with their need and desire to escape Allah's punishment. Muslims recognize that only Allah can grant a successful earthly life, and a successful eternal life in paradise. Consequently, believers know their *dua* will be granted only if Allah is on their side.

The way to know Allah is on the side of the

believer is to implement what Allah permits and not do what Allah says is unlawful like oppressing, usurping land, and denying human rights.

> **Verily the most honored of you in the sight of Allah is (he who is) the most righteous of you.**
>
> *Qur'an* 49:13

> **It is righteousness to believe in Allah and the Last Day and the angels and the Book and the Messengers; to spend of your substance out of love for Him for your kin, for your orphans, for the needy, for the wayfarer, for those who ask and for the ransom of slaves; to be steadfast in prayer and practice regular charity; to fulfill the contracts which ye have made; and to be firm and patient in pain (or suffering) and adversity and throughout all periods of panic. Such are the people of truth the God fearing.**
>
> *Qur'an* 2:177

Only when they obey these precepts do believers see their *dua* fulfilled. The relationship between Allah and his servants is conditional.

> **I listen to the prayer of every**

suppliant when he calleth on Me; let them also with a will listen to My call and believe in Me; that they may walk in the right way.

Qur'an 2:186

Often people in need ask others they hope are in a better relationship with their Creator to pray for them because they hope Allah will grant the request on their behalf. That is why the *dua* is such a powerful tool. When Sulayman (PBUH) made his *dua*, he submitted to Allah's call and strove to fulfill his end of the conditional relationship. That is proof positive that Allah's promise is real and unwavering! It also explains why the *dua* is a form of worship.

Muhammad (PBUH) said if the son of Adam were given a valley full of gold, he would never be satisfied because he would want a second, and if he got a second he would want a third. He would be so consumed with material wealth he would neglect enriching his spiritual essence. That shows that Sulayman's (PBUH) initial behavior was not unlike our behavior today. Yet he recognized his mistake and corrected it. By repenting, Sulayman (PBUH) not only acknowledged his shortcoming but also that Allah alone can satisfy us by curbing out natural desire for endless wealth. That is the next stage to pass: realize that we cannot overcome our weaknesses without Allah's assistance.

The final phase is to maintain consciousness and the activism that promotes it constantly, the stage of struggle against all opposing forces. Completing the previous stages proves one worthy of Allah's bounty. We cannot improve ourselves without recognizing that. To excel in any endeavor, our consciousness must be perpetual, permeate every facet of life. We must nourish it every day to combat the forces that embrace wrong and forbid right. Our consciousness must be advanced at every opportunity because the unjust forces never stop attacking. Consciousness must oppose any oppressive system, because the oppressors control newspapers, television and other means of propaganda.

This is why the *dua* is so important. The *dua* gives the weak and oppressed an equalizing force. The *dua* helps those oppressive societies call worthless. The *dua* defeats those who think themselves invincible. The *dua* gives victory to those society says have no hope. The *dua* gives power to those who use it justly.

No matter how many believers make a *dua*, the conditional relationship must be met to make the *dua* successful. If oppressors begin to make *duas*, they will eventually reach the same conclusion as Sulayman (PBUH) or they will fall as a result of their own actions. If they come to Sulayman's conclusion (PBUH), they will stop oppressing and clean up the society they have corrupted. Thus everyone benefits.

**O My Lord! Let my entry
be by the gate of truth and honour
and likewise my exit by the gate of**

**truth and honour; and grant me
from thy Presence an authority to
aid (me).**

Qur'an 17:80

That was Muhammad's (PBUH) *dua* when he was driven out of Mecca and fled to Medina. He was asking that his return to Mecca would be for the purpose of purging it from the idolatry and pagan community it had become. This shows that the prophets perfected what we must practice today, the technique of calling upon Allah in true faith to embrace difficulty and struggle. That is also a form of *dhikr* (remembrance of Allah). As Allah gave them strength and victory over their enemies in response to their *duas*, He will respond to ours the same way if we uphold our end of the conditional relationship. The power of *dua* emphasizes the difference between *ilm* and *iman* or knowledge and faith.

Knowledge and faith are easily confused. We defer to the prophets and messengers for every application of our way of life because they combined and exhibited excellent understandings of both aspects expertly. Many people today assume that if someone knows Arabic he understands the correct application of Allah's commands. Though Al-Islam originated in the east, people from there are not necessarily the most knowledgeable and pious.

The examples of Sulayman (PBUH) and the other prophets show us that no one can succeed by observing one characteristic without the other. The way to determine if people have true faith is to wait until hardship comes and observe how they handle it. Do they turn to Allah for strength, or do they turn somewhere else?

> **And certainly, We shall test you with something of fear hunger, loss of wealth, lives and fruits, but give glad tidings to the patient. Who when afflicted with calamity, say: "Truly to Allah we belong and to Him is our return. They are the ones on whom blessings are received from their Lord and receive His Mercy and it is they who are the rightly guided.**
>
> *Qur'an* 2:155-157

A person could be a *hafiz* (one who has memorized the entire *Qur'an*) yet think he need not struggle to live this way of life. Such people might think they need only to be a *hafiz* and devote all their time to that while ignoring the condition of oppressed people that need help. Some may dress like Prophet Muhammad (PBUH) but refuse to stand up for justice as he did. Some may recite the Qur'an beautifully yet mistreat their neighbors. All of these are examples of disconnects between *ilm* and *iman*. One reason Allah tests us is to show which of us are true with knowledge and faith in Him. A test maybe not only hardship but also a blessing since it gives Muslims a chance to show their faith—for which Allah will reward them: **"Verily with difficulty there is ease"** (*Qur'an* 94:5).

Anyone can reach that level of understanding, regardless of socioeconomic status. In many cases, those with nothing invested in a corrupt system often reach the highest degree of faith, while the rich without faith trust in their wealth instead of Allah. They may know all about Muhammad's (PBUH) customs and practices, but their love of wealth strips away their faith and commitment to Allah. Sulayman (PBUH) learned that lesson and never repeated his error.

Once his kingdom was restored, he used his wealth to further the message, *"La illaha Ill Allah"* (There is no god worthy of worship except God), and Allah continually blessed him with more wealth and power. People who come from poor and disadvantaged backgrounds should never despair. Society may turn its back on them, but Allah will not. They often surpass the wealthy in faith and knowledge. When a *dua* is made, it is with the intent of getting closer to Allah.

If needy people are more attached to things than to Allah, their *dua* will be seen for what it is, but if needy people are attached to the worship of Allah, they will be blessed in ways the rich do not comprehend. Thus does Allah redress the balance for the disadvantaged, the poor and the oppressed.

Allah has promised those

among you who believe, and do righteous good deeds, that He will certainly grant them succession to (positions of authority) in the earth, as He granted it to those before them, and that He will grant them the authority to practice their religion, that which He has chosen for them. And He will surely give them in exchange a safe security after their fear (provided) they (believers) worship Me and do not associate anything in worship with Me.

Qur'an 24:55

Muslims have been given a *dua* for everything we do—*duas* to be said when we look in the mirror, when we use the bathroom, when we travel or when given a compliment. That trains our souls to remember Allah constantly. If we train our souls, our minds and bodies follow. By remaining constant in this remembrance, we can improve conditions around us as Allah improves our internal conditions through His remembrance. If we practice this regularly, dealing with adversity becomes less difficult. This regular practice yields patience.

The supplication of the servant is granted in case he does not supplicate for sin or for severing the ties of blood, or he does not become impatient... Impatience means to say that he supplicated and he supplicated, but did not find it being responded, and then he becomes frustrated and abandons his supplication.

Prophet Muhammad (PBUH)

VALUE OF PATIENCE DURING STRUGGLE

> **By the token of time. Verily man is in loss, except those who believe and do righteous good deeds and recommend one another to the truth, and recommend one another to patience (for the sufferings, harms, and injuries which one may incur in Allah's Cause during preaching of Islamic monotheism).**
>
> *Qur'an:*103

This verse sums up what one who embraces the struggle against injustice can anticipate from the purveyors of injustice. It also provides a tool essential for rising above the tactics of the friends of tyranny and oppression: *sabr* or patience. Patience during struggle helps prevent uncontrolled spontaneous reactions that can harm the cause we struggle for. The best Qur'anic example of that patience is that of Prophet Ayub or Job (PBUH): **"Truly! We found him patient. How excellent (a) slave! Verily he was oft returning in repentance!"** (*Qur'an* 38:44).

Ayub (PBUH) had great wealth, cattle, good health, property and family, yet Ayub (PBUH) never became arrogant or haughty. In fact he increased his charity and prayed more to perfect his worship. He routinely bought slaves and freed them. He strove always to remember his Lord. He became more thankful, more intensely dedicated to pleasing his Lord. Many in his position would find little time to worship, but Ayub

(PBUH) dedicated more time to it.

Ayub's (PBUH) determination to worship more even after he grew rich angered Shaytan. He went first to Ayub (PBUH) and whispered about the good things in his life as he prayed. Ayub (PBUH) did not let the whispering distract him from his prayers. When his tactic failed, Shaytan complained to Allah that Ayub's (PBUH) dedicated worship was not sincere but meant only to satisfy Allah so he could hang onto his wealth. He suggested that if Allah (PBUH) stripped him of his wealth, Ayub (PBUH) would stop praising and glorifying his Lord. Allah replied that Ayub (PBUH) was his most devoted servant, that his worship was sincere, but to prove his point Allah gave Shaytan and his agents their way with Ayub's (PBUH) wealth.

Shaytan and his agents laid waste to Ayub's (PBUH) cattle, his servants and his lands until nothing was left. Then Shaytan took the form of a wise old man, went to Ayub and said that people were saying Allah took his wealth away to please Ayub's (PBUH) enemies. He implied that were Allah able to prevent harm, He would have protected Ayub (PBUH). Ayub (PBUH) replied that anything Allah takes away belongs to Him anyway and that it is for Allah to give and withhold from whom He pleases. Ayub (PBUH) said his only role was as a trustee to what Allah gave him.

When Shaytan heard that, he was infuriated. He went back to Allah and said Ayub (PBUH) was hiding his discontent, that he really valued his family. If Allah (PBUH) took his children from him, Ayub (PBUH) would lose faith. Allah said it would never happen but gave the Shaytan his way again.

Shaytan and his agents shook Ayub's (PBUH) children's home to the ground, and everyone inside died. He went to Ayub (PBUH) again, disguised as a sympathizer, bewailing his sad circumstances, saying Allah was unfair not to reward his dedicated worship. Ayub (PBUH) observed that sometimes Allah gives and sometimes He takes, but that he would remain faithful, regardless. Incensed, Shaytan reported to Allah that Ayub's (PBUH) wealth was gone, his children killed, yet he was still healthy. He argued that if he lost his health, Ayub (PBUH) would finally abandon worship. Allah denied it, but gave Shaytan authority over Ayub's (PBUH) body—though not his heart or mind, since they house the knowledge and remembrance of Allah.

Shaytan ravaged Ayub's (PBUH) body with severe diseases and reduced him to a mere shell, covered with scabs and sores. His condition was so horrible, everyone except his wife deserted him. Still Ayub (PBUH) remained faithful. Desperate, Shaytan finally went to Ayub's (PBUH) wife disguised as a man and reminded her of the days when she had wealth, family and health.

That sent her to Ayub (PBUH). She demanded that he tell Allah that it was all unacceptable and demand redress. Ayub (PBUH) compared their eighty years blessed with wealth, family and health to only seven years of suffering and told his wife to leave him alone if her faith were weak. Once alone, Ayub (PBUH) offered *dua* to Allah.

> **Verily! Shaytan has touched me with distress and torment!**
> *Qur'an* 38:41

> **Verily, distress has seized me and You are the Most Merciful of all those who show mercy.**
> *Qur'an* 21:83

Allah replied, "**Strike the ground with your foot: This is a spring of water to wash in, cool and a (refreshing) drink**" (*Qur'an* 38:42).

Ayub (PBUH) obeyed and immediately saw his excellent health restored as a result, and that was only the beginning.

> **And We gave him (back) his family, and along with them the like thereof, as a Mercy from Us and a reminder for those who understand.**
> *Qur'an* 38:43

Allah not only restored all Ayub's (PBUH)

losses but also gave him more! Note: Shaytan, his as-sistants and his human conspirators use the same tactics from generation to generation against those who stand up for Allah, defend justice and oppose oppression. Shaytan first whispered suggestions to Ayub (PBUH) to make him forget his commitment to Allah. When that did not work, Shaytan attacked his wealth. When that failed, Shaytan attacked his family and finally his body.

> **Secret counsels (conspira-cies) are only from Shaytan in order that he may cause grief to the be-lievers. But he cannot harm them in the least, except as Allah permits, and in Allah let the believers put their trust.**
>
> *Qur'an* 58:10

History shows that oppressors use the same strategy against anyone who resists. When we embrace the struggle against oppression, we must first decide what we value most. True freedom has a price. Before we enter the struggle we must understand that the more we struggle against oppression, the harder it may be to find a way to earn our living. The more we struggle, the more business a self-owned company may lose. The more business we lose, the less money we have. The less money, the greater the chance of poverty and strain upon our families. As we learn, **"And certainly, We shall test you with something of fear, hunger, loss** of wealth, lives and fruits, but give glad tidings to the patient" (*Qur'an* 2:155).

People who embrace struggle lay all their earthly riches and social standing on the line. They may find individuals who support their struggle quietly but are afraid to get involved publicly. Before embracing the struggle, we must make a conscious spiritual commitment to endure the tests lest we capitulate at the first sign of pain. Spiritual commitment is a discipline to prepare for future tests, the spiritual strength that trains our psyches to rise above enormous difficulties.

Discipline enabled Ayub (PBUH) to remain steadfast and become an example of what Allah means when He speaks of those who are patient. Spiritual training begins by devoting time out of our day to worshipping Allah. That accustoms the soul and heart to putting worship of Allah ahead of everything else every day. Once we observe that, embracing the struggle against oppression is easier. The need for sacrifice grows ever greater and more intense as a result.

The Muslim's prayers, like Ayub's (PBUH), condition the heart and soul. Humans naturally attach themselves to the familiar. The goal of spiritual training in Al-Islam is to attach ourselves to the familiar worship of Allah so that neither wealth nor oppressive governments can enslave us. Ayub's (PBUH) passion for Allah explains why the Shaytan's whisperings did not affect him. That passion should burn so strong in a person such that he would prefer to die standing on his feet as opposed to living on his knees.

> **Say: I seek refuge with (Allah) the Lord of mankind. The King of mankind. The God of mankind. From the evil of the whisperer (Shaytan who whispers evil in the hearts of men) who withdraws (from his whispering in one's heart after one remembers Allah) Who whispers in the breasts of mankind, of jinns and men.**
> *Qur'an* 114

Enemies of Al-Islam say Muslims pray too much or are too seriously dedicated to worship, that we should confine our worship of Allah to the *masjid* on Friday and leave it there. But how can we confine worship to one place and one day when the forces of oppression and tyranny work nonstop everywhere? Spiritual commitment trains Muslims to wage perpetual battle against the whisperings of drugs, alcohol, gambling and other indecencies.

> **Shaytan wants only to excite enmity and hatred between you with intoxicants and gambling, and hinder you from the remembrance of Allah and from prayer. So will you not then abstain?**

Qur'an 5:91

**Verily those who are pious,
when an evil thought comes to them
from Shaytan, they remember Allah
and they then see aright.**

Qur'an 7:201

When we struggle against injustice, if we can overcome the negative whisperings of a corrupt, cruel society or government, we soon focus on the society that pushes those vices onto our community, and society will attack our way of earning a living, as Shaytan did Ayub (PBUH). If our resolve holds, society will attack our families. It should come as no surprise that when the American military bombed Iraq in 2003 it killed many innocent women and children with its "precision smart bombs."

They refused to call this activity by its true name; murder, instead named it "shock and awe." The intended effect was to make the innocent men, women and children of that country suffer for opposing an unjust occupation submit to the power and might of a force that was killing them.

If targeting one's family is unsuccessful, then the body of the one actually resisting injustice will then become the next target. This is one of the reasons why those same bombs were laced with depleted uranium.

It would seep into the earth's soil, and water supply. Poisoning not only those who made up the resistance, but their families for future generations in order to ensure that as the occupation continued the resistance would eventually die out.

Such tactics failed to destroy Ayub's (PBUH) faith. Even though Shaytan brought affliction upon Ayub (PBUH) with Allah's permission, he could never attack Ayub's (PBUH) intellect, heart or soul. That is still true today.

> **So, when you want to recite the Qur'an, seek refuge with Allah from Shaytan, the outcast. Verily! He has no power over those who believe and put their trust only in their Lord. His power is only over those who obey and follow him, and those who join partners with Allah.**
>
> *Qur'an* 16:98-100

The story of Ayub (PBUH) shows us that another common mode of attack is to masquerade as a friend to get someone to let his defenses down. Shaytan approached Ayub (PBUH) disguised as the old man and the sympathizer. Ayub's (PBUH) patient perseverance gave him victory over them all. Patience worked for him, and it can work for anyone.

When we examine the condition of the Black

community and the crack epidemic, we see clearly that we need a higher level of spiritual commitment to prepare our community to rid neighborhoods of that poison. The solution lies in first ridding ourselves of those vices and mounting an organized movement concentrated on economic, social and political independence. Epidemics such as crack cocaine were directed towards the Black community to prevent this.

Spiritual training and patient perseverance like Ayub's (PBUH) are indispensable tools for anyone struggling to overcome injustice. That is why J. Edgar Hoover once said he "must prevent the rise of a black messiah." He understood that with the spiritual training practiced by prophets like Ayub (PBUH) Blacks could throw off the emotional and spiritual shackles that organized oppression advances. The entire community would then fight to throw off their physical shackles which existed in the form of lynchings, and Jim Crow laws. Hoover knew Blacks would naturally seek to take physical control of every facet of their community. The effect of such would be a serious upset of a power structure that spoke of the land of the brave, yet ensured it remained the home of the slave.

Oppressors can uproot any movement devoid of spiritual training, because oppressors know the oppressed can be co-opted and turned against their own best interests for material gain. A proper spiritual foundation, however, produces people who refuse to compromise the freedoms Allah gave them. A proper spiritual foundation can resonate with anyone across racial, ethnic and nationalistic lines. That was why Hoover used the spiritual word *messiah*: one who awakens consciousness in oppressed people. In other words, a proper spiritual foundation in Al-Islam as Ayub (PBUH) practiced would be a juggernaut against an oppressor.

Movements that stress only ethnic or race pride, however, appeal only to people of those racial groups but never to people outside them, despite their individual condition. As a result, such movements generate only a fraction of the speed and power they need to transform a bad revolution into a good one. That is why such organizations command mainstream media press coverage. The major news networks understand that giving attention to such groups actually marginalizes them and their appeal.

Movements based on the natural purpose all men were created for—to worship Allah—resonate with people across national lines and become international forces. That is what El Hajj Malik El Shabazz was trying to accomplish before he was martyred. Such movements have Allah's spiritual support to help them in the struggle against the forces of injustice, just as Ayub (PBUH) had. Mastery of fearing one's Creator is an indispensable and necessary quality in one's repertoire.

VALUE
OF
TRUE
TAQWA

Courage is the ability to do what is right and just despite pressure to do otherwise. *Taqwa* is exercising courage from fear of displeasing one's Lord. Injustice and oppression occur anytime someone violates another's humanity with impunity. Muslims cannot say they are believers unless they have the courage to stand against injustice. That is so because Allah decrees it.

> **O ye who believe! Stand out firmly for justice as witnesses to Allah, even as against yourselves, or your parents, or your kin, and whether it be against rich or poor. For Allah takes better care of both. Follow not the desires of your hearts, lest ye swerve, and if ye distort justice or decline to do justice, verily Allah is well acquainted with all that ye do.**
>
> *Qur'an* 4:135

Muhammad (PBUH) said that anyone who sees an act of injustice should "change it with his hands. If he can't do that he should speak against it. If he can't do that, he should hate it in his heart, and this is the weakest of faith."

Many Muslims choose the last option without attempting the first two out of fear of incurring their enemies' disfavor. To understand courage, we must examine the steps the Quraysh (the collection of powerful Meccan tribes that warred on Prophet Muhammad [PBUH] when he began to spread Al-Islam) took against the Islamic movement. First, they ignored the message of Al-Islam and hoped Muhammad (PBUH) would go away. When that didn't work, they used negative propaganda against him, called him a madman, a man possessed by demons, a soothsayer. When that didn't work they offered him money, power and influence to compromise and water down the message of Al-Islam. Muhammad's (PBUH) response was to say that if they put the sun in one of his hands and the moon in the other, he would never renounce this message.

When that didn't work, they offered to mutually worship Allah half the year and their pagan gods the other. Muhammad (PBUH) replied, **"Allah does not share His Command with anyone"** (*Qur'an* 18:26).

When that didn't work, the Quraysh instituted an economic boycott against all Muslims. Bank accounts were seized, and Muslim owned businesses were shut down. The Muslims' economic lifeline was completely cut off. When the Muslims refused to renounce Al-Islam, the tribes of Quraysh formed a coalition of the willing to try—unsuccessfully—to murder Muhammad (PBUH). In spite of all, Muhammad (PBUH) and the Muslims neither wavered in their faith nor buckled under the pressure to worship anything other than Allah. That is why Muhammad (PBUH) said the best of his *ummah* (community) were those in his generation.

Muslims must understand that the best of this life and the best of the hereafter are not free. Believers must wage constant struggle and sacrifice to prove themselves worthy of Allah's rewards. Without a *jihad* (constant struggle to worship Allah as He intended) as evidenced by Sheikh Uthman, we would not need courage. There would be no way to distinguish strong from weak, leaders from followers, friends of Allah from friends of Shaytan.

Several individuals find the word, *jihad* upsetting, and in an effort to not upset others have chosen to refrain from its use. I have chosen otherwise in order to disempower those who have corrupted the term and attempted to change its meaning. The word literally means to struggle. It does not mean to make war or to kill. Muslims must use all words and concepts that Allah uses in the Qur'an in the manner taught by the prophets and messengers whether well received or not. The messengers were not taught and did not teach that indiscriminate murder and mayhem was justified to spread any philosophy. Al Islam was the first ideology to stand for justice everywhere and against injustices such as oppression, slavery and racism. Al Islam and its adherents must advance this in spite of the forces that further their imperial agendas while practicing these methods.

**Those who believe and adopt
exile and struggle for the faith in the**

cause of Allah as well as those who
give them asylum and aid, these are
in very truth believers: for them is
the forgiveness of their sins and a
provision most generous.

Qur'an 8:74

We must understand that we cannot live anywhere without struggling to stand up for Al-Islam. That
is the nature Allah gave us. People naturally fear struggling against injustice, yet fear does not relieve us of
the obligation to resist it and advocate justice for the
oppressed, Muslim or otherwise.

When Allah ordered Musa (PBUH) to go to
Pharaoh and stand against his evil, Musa (PBUH) admitted his fear, then asked Allah to ease his struggle,
remove his speech impediment and give him a helper to
add strength to his own. Allah granted those requests
and told Musa (PBUH), **"But speak to him (Pharaoh)
mildly; perchance he may take heed or fear Allah"**
(*Qur'an* 20:44).

Musa (PBUH) knew he had been ordered to
comply with Allah's command, and Allah gave him the
help he needed. That is a lesson for all Muslims. If we
stand up for Al-Islam, stand against injustice and
tyranny instead of capitulating to our enemies, Allah
provides the tools we need for His cause to triumph.
That is the true meaning of *taqwa* or *fear of Allah*.

As long as Muslims fear incurring the wrath of Allah more than that of the enemies of truth and justice, Allah is always close at hand. The story of Uthman dan Fodio proves that. Allah's help is more powerful than any atomic bomb or technologically advanced weapon. Musa (PBUH) had no army, no weapons to match Pharoah's, yet he freed the slaves and instituted a system of justice in place of a tyranny. His only weapons were the words: *La illaha ill Allah*—there is none worthy of worship except God.

That explains why Prophet Muhammad (PBUH) said those words are light on the tongue but heavy on the scales of the Day of Judgment. He also reiterated that *the highest form of jihad is to speak truth to a tyrannical force.*

Physical force must counter physical oppression, but spiritual and psychological oppression precede physical oppression. That is why the tribes of Quraysh did not attack Prophet Muhammad (PBUH) physically at first. When Muhammad (PBUH) said that only Allah was worthy of worship, he affected the spiritual and psychological state of people trained in idolatry. Because the words *La illaha ill Allah* are so heavy, the tribes of Quraysh had no choice but to wage psychological war against Allah and His final prophet, Muhammad (PBUH). For the same reason Pharaoh called Musa (PBUH) a sorcerer and assembled his magicians against him. The intent was to sway the people away from the worship of Allah psychologically. Pharaoh knew he couldn't combat Musa (PBUH) spiritually.

In America orientalists attack Al-Islam by labeling all Muslims savages or terrorists while ignoring the terrorism of depleted uranium dipped bombs dropped on villages killing men, women, children and babies. The people who benefited from Pharoah's oppressive system had no problem supporting it as long as they were not its victims. As the Qur'anic story of Musa (PBUH) teaches, however, no system rooted in injustice can survive the test of time because it violates mankind's very essence, which is to be free to worship the Creator and not His creatures. Societies can thrive only on successful human conditions. If a society chokes its own citizens, it kills itself. Those lessons are evident when we view the life of not only Musa (PBUH), but also Lut or Lot (PBUH), Nuh or Noah (PBUH), and Isa or Jesus (PBUH).

Those men embodied the true meaning of courage and therefore were able to change an entire people's condition from slavery to strength and authority. They were not just prophets; they were prophet-revolutionaries! Yet their revolutions differed from all others because they used the concepts Allah taught them. His revelations and commands, not man-made concepts, brought about positive changes. Those men understood that man-made concepts include errors and fallacies because man is not perfect and repeats the same errors in various forms. If, however, we use concepts developed by an all-powerful, all-knowing perfect

Creator, then all are treated justly, because the Creator is worshipped instead of the creation!

Any revolution that does not understand that eventually becomes as oppressive as its predecessors, even if that is not its intent. Past revolutions demonstrate that. America fought the British in the Revolutionary War because of unjust taxation without representation. After America earned its independence, it oppressed Black people and used their forced labor to make America rich, though the Blacks had no share in the wealth their labor produced.

Patrick Henry eloquently articulated his desire for freedom in his speech *Give Me Liberty or Give Me Death* but had no qualms about denying the freedom he demanded for himself to the Blacks he owned. After America freed itself from the British yoke, it saw nothing wrong with waging war on those called Indians or the Mexicans to seize land that never belonged to it in the first place.

In our struggle against injustice and oppression, all Muslims must use the courage, the *taqwa,* of the prophet-revolutionaries. Allah said that He has made oppression unlawful for Himself and unlawful for us, that we all are liable to err except those He guides on the right path. We should seek right guidance from Him so He can direct us to the straight path. All hunger except those He feeds, so we should beg Him for food. All are naked except those for whom He provides garments, so we should beg Him for clothes. We cannot escape sin and error except that He is there to pardon us, so we should beg pardon from Him.

Everything society needs to succeed comes by Allah's permission. Food, clothing, shelter, justice and freedom from oppression all come from Allah. The prophet-revolutionaries had the courage to stand against injustice because they knew that. They recognized that to turn away from the struggle would be to say those gifts came from tyrants, not Allah. Musa (PBUH) knew if he cowered in fear of Pharaoh he would incur Allah's wrath.

Even though there can be no prophet or messengers of Allah after Prophet Muhammad (PBUH), anyone who follows his and the other prophets' footsteps can be a successful revolutionary any oppressor will come to hate and fear. That is why those who glorify themselves instead of Allah attack Al-Islam. They portray Al-Islam as a religion that teaches only hate and divisiveness in order to prevent Allah's message from reaching the rest of society.

The ones who claim that neglect to say that the prophet they claim to love and worship, Isa or Jesus (PBUH), hated oppression, tyranny and economic injustice. They ignore the fact that Jesus' teaching condemns their own behavior. The duty of every Muslim is to make that known without apology. Each Muslim must speak against the injustices he is powerless to change to combat the psychological campaign against Al-Islam and the oppressed masses. That is as much a part of the *Sunnah* as is eating with the right hand. All oppressive entities share the same characteristics.

An oppressive society must promote four things onto a people to maintain its injustice. Denial of human worth, ignorance, debt, and fear of the oppressor have been used since the beginning of time to ensure the survival of tyranny. A nation cannot be physically oppressed until it has been psychologically trained to devalue its own humanity. That is how Pharaoh enslaved the *Bani Israel* (Children of Israel) so long. That is how America maintained white supremacy over the Black people it enslaved. That is how Hitler tried to exterminate the entire European Jewish population. No tyrant begins physical oppression without laying the psychological foundation first.

As long as the people are kept ignorant of the system of justice their Creator designed for them, they will have no justification to resist oppression.

**For tyranny and oppression
are worse than slaughter.**
Qur'an 2:191

**And fight them on until there
is no more tumult or oppression and
there prevail justice and faith in
Allah.**
Qur'an 2:193

If an oppressed people are given this type of knowledge, they will prefer death to living under a system of injustice. They will resist with all of their possessions and their lives to prevent their progeny from suffering at the hands of tyranny.

> **Allah has promised, to those among you who believe and work righteous deeds, that He Will of a surety grant them in the land, inheritance of power as He has granted it to those before them: that He will establish in authority their religion- the one which He has chosen for them: and that He will change their state after the fear in which they lived, to one of security and peace. They will Worship Me alone and associate none with Me. If any do reject faith after this, they are rebellious and wicked.**
>
> *Qur'an* 24:55

As Muhammad (PBUH) said, many who are dirty and have unkempt hair and are turned away from doors (of access) are held in such high esteem by Allah that He will give them anything they ask in His name. That proves that Allah hates injustice and oppression and is automatically on the side of the oppressed who have faith in Him. If that knowledge is kept from people, however, they believe no one cares about them.

They abandon all hope of living in a just society. That is why it was so important to deprive the Blacks brought to America as slaves of Al-Islam.

Since money is essential to financial success, it makes sense that a society without proper finances cannot improve its infrastructure. By issuing loans at rates people must work for four generations to pay off, an oppressive society guarantees they will never be financially independent. It ensures they will never be able to decide how to spend their own money. Oppressors keep people in debt to ensure that families suffer while the oppressors benefit. They use debt to keep people enslaved for the rest of their lives.

Fear of the oppressor keeps people from standing up for themselves, makes them relinquish the rights that come from the Creator. Oppressors must portray themselves as the *only* ones who can protect, the *only* ones who can forgive, the *only* ones who can punish people to instill a false sense of worship of the oppressor in the minds of the oppressed.

If the oppressed believe that, they cooperate subconsciously with their oppressors. If, however, the oppressed worship Allah, the *only* one who can forgive, the *only* one who can protect, the *only* one who can punish, they do not fear resisting oppression. Neither their children nor their children's children will be afraid. They prefer death fighting oppression to a miserable life under it. They are assured to be rewarded in the next life for their struggle. They prefer the struggle to a life of slavery.

That is why oppressors must portray Al-Islam as a backward, foreign religion. If the masses understand Al-Islam as something Allah intends for the entire world, few will oppose it, and systems of injustice will fall. African Muslims ruled Spain for nearly eight centuries, bringing culture and agricultural advancement to Europe and allowing Jews to maintain their synagogues and Christians, their churches. Yet that is never mentioned. When Salahudin beat the crusaders and reconquered Jerusalem, instead of slaughtering Christians, he let them go in an act of peaceful mercy. Yet those who claim they are not at war with Al-Islam never mention it.

When Umar, the second caliph in Al-Islam and companion of Muhammad (PBUH), took possession of Jerusalem, the Christian king wanted him to pray in the church. Umar refused because he feared the Muslims would turn that church into a *masjid.* All are examples of people who fought against injustice and tyranny using the fear of Allah, yet they also practiced humility and mercy in reverence of that same fear.

Each Muslim's duty is to use the revelations of Allah to educate people of their worth to humanity, to replace ignorance with the correct knowledge of Allah's intended social order. Each Muslim must get out of debt and promote financial independence. Each Muslim must exchange fear of the oppressor for fear of Allah. So did the prophet-revolutionaries, and each Muslim inherits that legacy when they take *Shahadah* (the declaration of faith making one a Muslim). This is the *jihad* that never goes away. This is the basis of *jihad* from which one earns respect. This is what lets a woman know her husband can and will protect their family and community. That is what lets communities know their leaders are strong and worthy of support. This is what makes an oppressor know that if he attempts to annihilate an entire nation or community, he will receive an equal if not superior amount of formidable resistance upon him.

When Muslims do not speak out against oppression and injustice, they create an impression in the minds of some that Al-Islam has no position against these. That promotes passivity in an environment requiring action, promotes and rewards cowardice instead of courage. If the enemies of Al-Islam encourage Muslims to denounce actions Al-Islam does not support, these Muslims should be equally more encouraged by the party of Allah to denounce acts reprehensible to Al-Islam committed by the friends of oppression.

It is easy to understand why Muslims are afraid of this. Yet Musa (PBUH) was also afraid. However, a major difference between the prophet-revolutionary concept and weak Muslims today is that the prophet-revolutionaries used *taqwa* to inspire themselves to stand up for justice and earn an invitation to Allah's paradise.

The next verse encompasses the proper perception a person fighting injustice must have when standing against all odds.

> **If Allah helps you no one can overcome you: If He forsakes you, who is there after that, that can help you? In Allah then, let the believers put their trust.**
>
> *Qur'an* 3:160

A man fights for pride and haughtiness, another fights for bravery, and another fights for showing off . . . but the one who fights that Allah's Word (Al-Islam) should be superior, fights in Allah's Cause.

Prophet Muhammad (PBUH)

VALUE
OF
DEFYING
ODDS

Most are familiar with the story of David and Goliath or Daud (PBUH) and Jalut, though few are aware of the deep significance behind it. Its meaning is a necessity for anyone engaged in struggle.

Daud (PBUH) was not merely a courageous youth. He had been devoted to the worship of Allah his entire life, and Allah commissioned him as a prophet in Al-Islam. The point must be emphasized because it was not merely Daud (PBUH) who killed the giant Jalut with a slingshot, but it was Allah's help that came as a result of his devout worship. That was the key to Daud's (PBUH) victory, all too often overlooked. The story of Daud (PBUH) is crucial to all who have tried to overcome tough challenges.

Al-Islam adopts several strategies to win struggles. First, when Jalut saw Daud (PBUH) he not only mocked him but also reminded him of his lack of military prowess and physical strength. He boasted he would kill Daud (PBUH) easily and painfully. Oppressors always remind those who stand for justice of the odds against them. The purpose is to intimidate and discourage freedom fighters. They in turn must accept that they have nothing near the weapons and power oppressors have. Remaining conscious of that helps those resisting oppression strategize according to their own capacity and means.

El Hajj Malik El Shabazz once said that an oppressed people should *never* struggle within the framework developed by the oppressor, because ultimately the system of oppression becomes stronger while the oppressed get weaker.

Oppressors remind the oppressed of the odds against them, since that makes them easier to control, so the oppressed must analyze the oppressive system to determine where and how it can be used against itself. Historical analysis helps determine the oppressors' weaknesses that can be used against them. That is what Daud (PBUH) did.

He used Jalut's arrogance to make him doubt Allah's power and His ability to help His servants. Daud (PBUH) also let the physically more powerful Jalut think the fight would be the way he wanted it. Daud (PBUH), however, fought with the weapon most advantageous to *him*—the slingshot. Jalut, used to fighting with physical might and the sword, thought himself invincible since no man had yet beaten him.

We see examples of that in today's events also. In late 2005 the French government passed a law enabling employers to terminate workers under the age of twenty-six without cause. In response, French youth protested by marching, shutting down airports, train stations and bus systems, and paralyzing the government's ability to run the country. Eventually they forced the president to rescind the law.

The youths who took to the streets had no

army, no power to legislate, but they used the tools familiar to *them* and prevented a grave injustice being enacted upon them. Before the youths took the streets, the French government said rescinding the law was impossible, and the government had the final say. France's youths proved otherwise.

Second is the matter of fearing consequences. Daud (PBUH) knew quite well he could have been killed, but he refused to let fear control him. He ignored it. The operative question is how did Daud (PBUH) ignore the fear other more powerful men could not?

So they routed them by Allah's Leave and David killed Goliath, and Allah gave him the kingdom and wisdom, and taught him of that which He willed. And if Allah did not check one set of people by means of another, the earth would indeed be full of mischief.

Qur'an 2:251

Daud's (PBUH) belief in that verse let him overcome fear. Allah prevents injustice by raising the just above the unjust. To secure Allah's assistance, Daud (PBUH) knew he had to establish a track record of obedience to Allah. He had been trained to worship Allah from birth, so he had already a commitment to Allah unlike any other man's of his time. When Jalut challenged someone to face him, all other men refused, but because Daud (PBUH) understood Allah's will, his fear vanished.

Anyone who wants to understand the Qur'an must also understand how the prophets used it. The Qur'an and the way the prophets used it can never be separated. Daud (PBUH) exemplified that.

Third, when Daud (PBUH) volunteered to face Jalut, his own king tried to dissuade him, said he was not qualified, but because of his lifetime of devotion to Allah, he did not need anyone else's backing. He had what strengthens people to stand resolutely against injustice.

When faithful people reach that level, even if they are hurt in the struggle, they are freer than their adversaries. They inspire fear in their enemies. When Daud (PBUH) killed Jalut, the giant's army fled the battlefield in fear. Did they fear the young man? No, they feared the power of Allah working through the devoted young servant.

> **O Prophet! Urge the believers to fight. If there are twenty steadfast amongst you, they will overcome two hundred, and if there be a hundred steadfast they will overcome a thousand of those who disbelieve, because they are people who do not understand.**
>
> *Qur'an* 8:63

Such faith makes a seven year old Palestinian child throw rocks at Israeli tanks, knowing he could be killed. Such faith makes Nigerians fight to prevent British and American based petroleum companies from stealing their nation's oil wealth. Such faith strengthened Muhammad Ali to refuse in fighting an unjust war in Vietnam and instilled an active consciousness in other Americans to do the same. Consequently, he went from being the most hated man in America to being one of the world's most beloved men. All are examples of Allah's power at work. Such faith gave them and other oppressed peoples the might to resist any tyranny.

The American government hates Al-Islam for numerous reasons. Chiefly, Al-Islam does not accept total unjust subjugation by a bully. The most active resistance to the transatlantic slave trade came from African Muslims. One of several major slave rebellions occurred in 1835 in Bahia, Brazil, and Al-Islam played an important role in its organizing.

Mohammad Abdullah Hasan is another example of Allah's help for oppressed people. He was a Somali Muslim who opposed British and Italian imperialist armies simultaneously and defeated them all, in spite of fighting with deficient military technology and outnumbered troops. He not only beat the colonial powers but also remains a great source of strength and honor for the people of Somalia. His enemies so feared him that he was dubbed the "mad mullah." That emphasizes the fact that oppressors will deride anyone who refuses to accept colonialism as a way of life.

El Hajj Malik El Shabazz said that the worst leaders have the approval of those they oppose. He repeatedly emphasized that when he talked about how the media and White liberals identified what they called "responsible" leaders for the Black community. He pointed out that racist America called them responsible as they cared about obtaining the approval of racist America more than organizing the indigent masses for political, social and economic independence.A

There is also the example of Nasir Al Din. In the late 1600s he organized a movement against the slave trade that expanded from Mauritania to Senegal. He united all the region's tribes on the basis of Al-Islam. His organizational and leadership skills were so exceptional that the French could not capture slaves there as long as Muslims remained united in battling the slave trade. These important pieces of history emphasize the need for the removal of Al-Islam from Black people who were unjustly enslaved in America.

We should remember these stories whenever we face insurmountable odds. The oppressors know them well and many others like them. That is why in any struggle there must be an independent educational system. That is why Muhammad (PBUH) set up a school immediately after he established the *masjid* in Medina: to teach humanity that each community must control what its children learn. He also taught that educators must come from within the community that needs educating to insure that education is not devoid of compassion and understanding. Often when educators who are not from the community teach the youth, they fail to understand the intricate and intimate dynamics associated with the community and how they affect children's learning.

The Qur'an is filled with numerous examples of community life and stories of messengers and prophets sent to them. Allah also says that all prophets and messengers came from the communities to which they were sen

All too often people are eager to defer to those who come from outside their communities before attempting to work with those at home first. That makes young people lose confidence in and despise their own. They come to believe their own community has always been and will always be inferior. Once the young have that attitude, it is extremely difficult to expunge. Minds so affected ordinarily think negatively of their own communities.

When that mind must deal with any aspect concerning his community it will have a negative meaning. This is known as the inferiority complex. More will be discussed on that later.

The story of Daud (PBUH) shows that each community must stand up for itself, handle its own problems and protect its own interests. The story of Daud

(PBUH) shows that everyone must encourage themselves in the face of universal opposition. People everywhere should look to themselves before turning to others.

After several years, Allah finally gave Muhammad (PBUH) permission to fight the abuse he endured at the hands of the Quraysh. He immediately appointed generals and military leaders from within his own ranks, some with no prior military experience. As a result, many Muslims lacked confidence in their ability to lead effectively. Muhammad (PBUH) knew the only way to overcome their doubts was to let the people show themselves they could overcome anything, including their own self-doubts, with Allah on their side.

Leaders, especially from oppressed communities, must learn to overcome self-doubt to face their community's doubt about them. This way things that seem impossible to others will be extremely possible for them. This understanding leads to another aspect of developing wisdom.

VALUE
OF
GAINING
WISDOM
THROUGH
EXPERIENCE

The Qur'an teaches that we are to reflect and ponder all things explained.

> **Verily We have sent it down as an Arabic Qur'an in order that you may understand. We relate unto you the best of stories through Our Revelations unto you, of this Qur'an. And before this, you were among those who knew nothing about it.**
>
> *Qur'an* 12:2-3

From the story of Yusuf or Joseph (PBUH) we learn valuable lessons that apply to Muslims who are attacked and jailed for doing what is right, often to prevent the truth from surfacing. A married woman tried to seduce him, but he refused out of *taqwa*. The woman falsely accused him of a rape attempt and had him thrown in prison when he actually refused her advances: **"Then it occurred to them, after they had seen the proofs (of his innocence), to imprison him for a time"** (*Qur'an* 12:35).

She was no ordinary woman without authority but the wife of a very powerful chief minister with high social standing and influence in the society. She wanted something from Yusuf (PBUH) he would not give her because he feared displeasing his Lord.

Many people today are thrown in prison by powerful governments, not because of unjust criminal acts, but to prevent the government from having to deal with the consequences of its own corruption. Oppressive societies regularly require the oppressed to surrender their humanity to let oppression flourish. By jailing innocent people, oppressors instill fear to prevent others from organizing and uniting against their wickedness. The most recent example of this is that of Imam Jamil Al Amin, the former H. Rap Brown.

Originally coming to prominence in the Black Liberation Movement, he served in organizations such as the Nonviolent Action Group and eventually became the national chairman of the Student Nonviolent Coordinating Committee (SNCC). He performed duties aimed at helping Blacks overcome the racial injustices that had become synonymous with American life. Organizing voter registration drives in his early days to creating a spiritually vibrant community in one of Atlanta's most poverty stricken areas were just a few ways that he worked against oppression. Consequently, he became a target of the federal government.

In March of 1968, FBI director J. Edgar Hoover circulated a confidential memo to his agents naming four individuals he felt had the potential of becoming a "black messiah." His objective of this new counterintelligence program (COINTELPRO) endeavor was to "expose, disrupt, misdirect, discredit, or otherwise neutralize" any and all individuals supporting, Martin Luther King, Maxwell Stanford, Stokely Carmichael, and H. Rap Brown. These individuals were targeted in order to prevent the mass organization of the oppressed. One month after this memo Dr. King would be killed by an assassin's bullet.

H. Rap Brown eventually accepted Al Islam in the 1970s and changed his name to Jamil Abdullah Al Amin while in prison. Upon his release, he moved to Atlanta's west end and built an Islamic community becoming its *imam* or spiritual leader. He was successful in turning drug dealers and other criminals into productive positive citizens using Al Islam. Neighborhood residents would often remark as to how safe they felt when the Muslims were present. Several people would routinely seek his help in resolving a myriad of personal problems and social concerns. However the government harassment still persisted. This culminated in March of 2000 when two officers named Ricky Kinchen and Aldranon English were shot trying to serve an arrest warrant on Imam Jamil after he failed to appear in court concerning a traffic stop. Ricky Kinchen was fatally shot while Aldranon English survived. The police immediately identified Imam Jamil as the assailant. He was later apprehended, tried, convicted and sentenced to life without parole. However, there are certain inconsistencies that were overlooked during the trial and still continue today.

According to Deputy English, he shot the assailant. When other officers arrived at the scene they reported seeing a trail of blood leading to a vacant house. As a result the police told the public and the media reported the suspect to be a wounded Imam Jamil. When arrested, the police found no gunshot wounds or injuries whatsoever on him. When this was made public, the police stated the trail of blood was old and therefore deemed irrelevant. Deputy English testified seeing the assailant's grey eyes. Imam Jamil's eyes are brown. 911 tapes confirming reports of a wounded person in the area on the night in question were not admitted into evidence. Imam Jamil's fingerprints were not found on any weapon associated with the crime. Additionally, a man named Otis Jackson has repeatedly confessed to committing the crime since 2000. In spite of this, Imam Jamil has not been given a new trial, but has since been transferred to a super maximum security prison in Florence, CO without cause and without federal charges where he is currently kept in total isolation.

If the goal of a civilized government that exports democracy around the world is to ensure justice, does not that same justice entail ensuring one's guilt before punishment? Ruben "Hurricane" Carter was found guilty of three murders, but was eventually released after it was proven the New Jersey state government hid evidence confirming his innocence. He lost nearly 20 years of his life in prison. Elmer "Geronimo" Pratt was found guilty of murder after having been targeted by COINTELPRO. He served 27 years in prison before his conviction was overturned for similar reasons. Imam Jamil deserves a new trial at minimum, and a full investigation of all evidence that is currently being omitted. The story of Yusuf (PBUH) mirrors Imam

Jamil. Yet as Yusuf (PBUH) never wavered in faith or hope, neither does the imam. I believe one of the reasons for his transfer to a super maximum facility is to instill a psychological fear that can adversely impact his faith and extinguish the hope of all those opposing injustice. Thus far, Imam Jamil's attitude has remained similar to Yusuf (PBUH).

In spite of the endured hardship Yusuf's (PBUH) attitude was one that shocked even the ruler's wife. He said:

> **O my Lord! Prison is dearer to me than that to which they invite me. Unless you turn away their plot from me, I will feel inclined towards them and be one of the ignorant.**
>
> *Qur'an* 12:34

Yusuf (PBUH) preferred prison because he knew the alternative would incur his Lord's anger. He knew that prison would give him time to better his worship, to remember his blessings and to remind himself that he was being tested.

> **Be sure We shall test you with something of fear and hunger, some loss in goods or lives or the fruits (of your toil) but give glad tidings to those who patiently persevere.**
>
> *Qur'an* 2:155

In prison Yusuf (PBUH) perfected the miracles of accurately interpreting dreams which Allah blessed him with. Only a true prophet or messenger of Allah can interpret dreams correctly. Two men from the ruler's household were also in jail with Yusuf (PBUH). He not only interpreted their dreams but also increased the call to Al-Islam by inviting them to embrace the worship of Allah. Yusuf (PBUH) understood that they had neglected Allah and instead worshipped false deities while in the ruler's service.

Muhammad (PBUH) said that people who see dreams they like should talk about them. If they dream something they dislike, they should turn on the other side, blow to the left three times, seek refuge with Allah from the evil and tell no one.

Only people who worship Allah and refrain from worshiping other gods can understand that. That is why the two men went to Yusuf (PBUH) for interpretation of their dreams. Worshiping other gods with Allah limits our understanding and puts us in a spiritual state of oppression. That is why Yusuf (PBUH) called them to the worship of Allah. That is also why many people in prison enter the realm of Al-Islam. They want to expand their understanding and gain physical freedom which cannot be achieved without a spiritual awakening. Yusuf (PBUH) called them to worship Allah and was able to prove that his own faith had not wavered.

He also knew upon their release the men would

report to the king that worshiping other gods with Allah was not healthy for his kingdom. He proved that, though he was in prison, Allah blessed him with a power greater than the king's, something the king himself would realize later.

Soon, the king had a dream which depicted seven fat cows eaten by seven lean cows, seven green peaks of grain and others that were dry. None in his kingdom could interpret this dream. Finally, one of the former prisoners that knew Yusuf (PBUH), remembered his ability and informed the king of this. The man went to the prison, where Yusuf (PBUH) explained that the seven fat cows represented seven years of harvest and fertility of the land. This would be followed by seven years of drought. Once the drought had passed, there would come one year of rain during which the people would press wine and oil as usual.

When informed of this interpretation, the king immediately sent for Yusuf (PBUH) to be released, but Yusuf (PBUH) insisted on his good reputation and innocence being restored before he left prison. The king's wife finally admitted the truth and as compensation, the king allowed Yusuf (PBUH) to choose what position of authority he wanted to have. Yusuf (PBUH) chose to rule over all the supply warehouses in the land as minister of Egypt.

One day his brothers came to the warehouse seeking food, where he recognized them, but not them he. He gave them the food they requested upon the condition they return with their brother from their father's side. He allowed them to leave with their food after returning their money. When the brothers returned with their requested sibling, Yusuf (PBUH) secretly revealed his true identity to his brother, and told him to guard his identity.

He then allowed all of his brothers to leave, but not before ordering his servants to place a valuable cup in his brother's bag. He then ordered his servants to stop the caravan on their way home and detain the one in possession of the cup. When the brothers informed their father Yaqub (PBUH) of this he became so wrought with grief he went blind. Grieving for Yusuf (PBUH) and his son Binyamin or Benjamin he immediately ordered them to return to Egypt and find out what happened to both.

The men returned to Yusuf (PBUH) where he finally revealed himself by saying:

> **Do you know what you did with Yusuf and his brother when you were ignorant? They said, "Are you indeed Yusuf?" He said, "I am Yusuf" and this is my brother. Allah has certainly favored us. Indeed he who fears Allah and is patient, then indeed Allah does not allow to be lost the reward of those who do**

good." They said, "By Allah, certainly has Allah preferred you over us, and indeed we have been sinners." He said, "No blame will there be upon you today. Allah will forgive you; and He is the most merciful of the merciful. Take this, my shirt and cast it over the face of my father; he will become seeing. And bring me your family all together."

Qur'an 12:89-93

When people in prison find Al-Islam, they should use the time as Yusuf (PBUH) did. Muslims in prison must know that Allah will test their faith and should worship more to compensate for physical restriction: **"Verily with every difficulty there is relief."** (*Qur'an* 94:6). The relief may be the *sakinah* or tranquility Allah gives the believer's soul and heart in physical difficulty. Fighters of injustice usually emerge from prison more committed to the struggle against wrong than before imprisonment. Unjust systems use jail to break the prisoner's spirit. That reinforces the need for an established relationship with Allah.

When a tyrant sees an opportunity to neutralize his enemy, his opponents see an opportunity to get closer to Allah. Allah gives authority to those who prove themselves worthy of His blessings.

Yusuf's (PBUH) story is also significant because his own brothers sought to murder him due to their envy of their father's affection for him. Instead of treating their father better, or unifying the family, they chose to split the family by getting rid of their brother. Years later, when Yusuf (PBUH) saw them all together, instead of punishing them, he united them. He harbored no animosity or anger, only love and forgiveness. Similarly, the families of the wrongly imprisoned are also separated. Yusuf's (PBUH) example shows a way to rise above that.

The faith of he and his father Yaqub or Jacob (PBUH) prove how a family can remain together in spirit during difficulty. Oppressors want unity in oppression, they love to break up families. Yet without families, children will not be raised with the support system they need. Without the families, there is no community. Without community nothing can oppose injustice. Due to the strain of an unjust situation sometimes the families of prisoners disassociate themselves from one another. However, the bond that remained between Yusuf (PBUH) and Yaqub (PBUH) shows that does not have to be the case.

After Yusuf (PBUH) endured hardship, Allah rewarded him by releasing him from prison and giving him power over the very system that imprisoned him. His reputation was intact, his honor vindicated. He acquired wisdom with Allah's help and reunited his family. Exercising patience and wisdom in understanding

Allah's purpose helps us improve our response to every situation. Others see that and seek the company of the wise. All serve to give the message of Al-Islam a better reception, establish trust between people and foster cohesion and unity.

Yusuf (PBUH) had many lessons to learn. He had to learn how to overcome his brothers' envy. He also had to rise above the plots of those who imprisoned him. By withstanding the tests, he earned the responsibility to exercise power effectively. By proving himself to Allah, Yusuf (PBUH) proved he would not sacrifice the worship of Allah to his own interest. Allah gave him authority over his envious brothers and lifted him above the plots of all his enemies. Here are lessons for all who struggle against injustice similarly.

First, some may hate you only because you worship Allah. Often those nearest you are the harshest opponents. In addition, you may face the prospect of prison without knowing the exact reason. The American government today has imprisoned people without charging them with a crime. José Padilla was in jail more than three years before the government officially charged him. Never mind that the final charge had nothing to do with the original reasons they stated for locking him up. Never mind that only pressure from the Supreme Court to decide the matter moved the government to finally issue a charge against him.

Such tactics are nothing new. The story of

Yusuf (PBUH) shows this to be an ancient practice. Allah vindicated Yusuf (PBUH) and gave him victory over his enemies. Time after time Allah has proven He supports those who struggle against injustice and oppression today. This is an aspect of believing in the Unseen. We cannot see Allah, but we know from past events that He never forsakes those who worship Him. Muslims in prison should use the time to grow spiritually. The prison environment can be that training ground, as it was for Yusuf (PBUH).

People who embrace Al-Islam and face hostility from their families should not be upset but rather exuberant because Allah has set them on the same path as righteous Muslims like Yusuf (PBUH). Perhaps Allah wants to reward them with power and authority like Yusuf (PBUH). Righteous people who are unjustly punished know Allah will lift them above hardships in this life and the hereafter.

> **O ye who believe! Stand out firmly for Allah as witnesses to fair dealing and let not hatred of others to you make you swerve to wrong and depart from justice. Be just: that is next to piety: and fear Allah for Allah is well acquainted with all that ye do.**
>
> *Qur'an 5:8*

And O my people! Give just

measure and weight nor withhold from the people the things that are their due: commit no evil in the land with intent to do mischief.

Qur'an 11:85

Going to prison for embracing good and forbidding wrong is not shameful but honorable in the sight of Allah.

Say My Lord hath commanded justice; and that ye set your whole selves (to Him) at every time and place of prayer and call upon Him making your devotion sincere as in His sight: such as He created you in the beginning so shall ye return.

Qur'an 7:29

As this verse is implemented, methods geared to supporting the release of those who are imprisoned unjustifiably should be developed. This action reinforces their faith in Allah, and it reassures them that others understand, sympathize and care about their condition. They literally have the full weight of an entire government on top of them to keep them wrongfully imprisoned. It feels good to the soul, when others try to relieve some of that burden.

Refusal to support deserving individuals does not build a community. It is the very antithesis of community building, since the message is, "We are with you until we can no longer derive benefit from you." There is no mutual give and take. This is why *sadaqa* (optional charity) is so important in Al- Islam. For people to receive *sadaqa*, someone must give it. If no one gives, no one receives. If no one receives, a class division between people opens and greed becomes the order of the day. Greed ultimately retards human development.

All oppressed people should be able to relate to Yusuf (PBUH). Those nearest him betrayed him. His own brothers abandonment allowed him to be sold into slavery. Finally, he was imprisoned unjustly. Those who benefit from the suffering of others often say, "All they have to do is work hard, do the right things like I did and they will succeed." Yet they ignore the horrible conditions the oppressed constantly endure. Yusuf (PBUH) did everything to please Allah, but the forces of evil conspired against him. Yusuf (PBUH) proved that oppressed people can triumph with Allah's help in spite of evils like racism and bigotry, not because they do not exist.

Someone once asked Muhammad (PBUH), "Who is the most worthy of respect among the people?" He said, "The most God-fearing, and that the most honorable person was Yusuf, Allah's prophet, the son of Allah's prophet (Yaqub), the son of Ibrahim, Allah's faithful friend."

Reap the rewards of learning wisdom from

your experiences. The experiences of Yusuf (PBUH) helped him succeed. Black people in America and Africa should never feel unworthy because of the oppression that is part of their human experiences but rather use those experiences to excel. The resolve that was produced as a result of suffering is one part of their rich legacy. Anyone who does not respect your legacy does not deserve the honor of being your student and definitely not your teacher!

A key to overcoming oppression is to value what Allah values and to reject what Allah rejects. That ensures you will never devalue your own humanity. It does not matter what others think of you, because you know what Allah expects, demands and authorizes. Regardless of the negative images society paints, you will not have a negative image of yourself. As people capitulate to injustice, they accept the oppressive system. The will to resist is crushed, mental, psychological and emotional fortitude stifled. Without them, existence is empty.

People who succumb to oppression are powerless to determine their own affairs. They beg the oppressor to recognize their humanity and give them what should be given only to Allah. They abandon the struggle of the oppressed to become part of the oppressing system in exchange for an expensive car or house in the oppressor's neighborhood.

O mankind! Reverence Your

Guardian Lord Who created you from a single person, created of like nature His mate, and from them twain scattered (like seeds) countless men and women fear Allah, through Whom ye demand your mutual rights.

Qur'an 4:1

For everything we possess we owe thanks to Allah. The air we breathe, the water we drink and the justice we dispense come from Him. Regardless of technological advancements, water has been and will always be two parts hydrogen and one part oxygen. No matter how much we think of our talents, we will never change that formula. We will never be able to outperform Allah. When we think we can, we disturb the order Allah created the universe in.

As Allah created justice to preserve the system of order, man must uphold that justice if he is to survive. Oppression denies this justice. When someone steals from an orphan, that is oppression. When spouses refuse to recognize their mate's rights over them, that is oppression. When people are thrown in prison unjustly, that too is oppression. The American legal system's slogan is *Equal justice under the law.* That means regardless of race or status, no one is to be denied justice. Yet all too often we see the poorest, often the darkest, penalized because they cannot invest in the system to prevent it from victimizing them.

Sentences Served for Different Classes of Crime 1996-1997		
Crimes of the poor	Average Time Served (in months)	Percent Sentenced to Prison
Robbery	99	60
Burglary	89	28
Auto Theft	63	24
Crimes of the affluent		
Fraud	63	16
Tax Law Violation	42	15
Embezzlement	58	9
The Rich Get Richer and the Poor Get Prison (Sixth Edition) *Pg 135*		

All oppressive systems lock the oppressed out of opportunities reserved for oppression's partners. The oppressed often see crime as a way of evening the score by taking some of the oppressor's wealth. That is why the previous chart is significant and also why *zakat* is so important in Al Islam. The affluent *have to* support the poor. *Zakat* teaches the poor that society cares for them and will never abandon them as the American government abandoned the predominantly poor Black victims of Hurricane Katrina. Other examples of unjust disparities abound.

In November 2003, millionaire Robert Durst was acquitted of a murder he admitted. He shot Morris Black and dismembered his body with an ax, hid the victim's head and meticulously cleaned up the crime scene. Yet in November 2005, Harold C. Wilson, a Black man, was released from prison after serving seventeen years, mostly on death row, for three murders committed in 1989. He was proven innocent of all charges in 2005 when DNA evidence exonerated him. A system that claims to extend justice to all should not tolerate such things.

The crimes of the affluent listed on the previous chart are just a small example showing that some who have privilege and status at the expense of others are never satisfied until they consolidate more. While both categories of crimes are unjustified, the same conditions of being a victim on one hand and a victimizer on the other explain why they take place in an oppressive society.

After Yusuf (PBUH) interpreted the king's dream, he was freed, but he refused to leave prison until his innocence was established. He totally rejected the system of oppression and injustice. He refused to acquiesce to tyranny at any time because he knew that to give in at all would mean enslavement. This is how the story of Yusuf (PBUH) should inspire all who have ever found themselves in the ranks of the oppressed. Yusuf (PBUH) also showcases strength in a condition none wish for themselves: standing alone.

VALUE
OF
STANDING
ALONE

To please Allah requires strength, courage and independent thought. Allah's great prophets mastered those virtues. In the Qur'an, Allah details how the prophets went against the status quo to perform His will. A good example is Lut or Lot (PBUH).

Lut (PBUH) lived where homosexual behavior was widely practiced and accepted. Allah ordered Lut (PBUH) to convey His displeasure about the matter. Not even Lut's (PBUH) wife supported his mission, unlike Khadijah, Muhammad's (PBUH) wife and first supporter. Family support was critically important to all the prophets. Imams today rely on their wives to provide the emotional nourishment and support they need to deal with problems in their communities.

Unfortunately, Lut (PBUH) did not have it. Not only did his wife not support him, but she also collaborated against his mission! Lut (PBUH) never had a single moment of rest or relaxation. He could easily have capitulated to the accepted behavior, but his commitment was so strong, he neither needed nor wanted society's approval. As a result the citizens isolated, castigated, mocked and abused him. He endured all and escaped the punishment Allah inflicted on the community.

That should be a lesson to those who are afraid to defend Al-Islam from fear of losing their standing in society. Lut's (PBUH) struggle lasted years, not days. People who consider taking a stand for the truth should know they may have to suffer and be willing to pay the price. When Allah sent angels in the form of men to Lut's (PBUH)) home to warn him of the impending punishment and tell him to take his family to safety, the struggle intensified. The people attacked Lut (PBUH) because he protected these visitors from them. He preferred fighting the entire town to letting his visitors be violated. Such determination, willingness and strength cannot come from earthly support. That is what makes Lut (PBUH) unique.

Those who sacrifice and endure patiently receive far greater rewards than those who sit back. The act of standing alone is the culmination of something greater that burns deep within the soul, a fire within that radiates toward everyone who sees someone take a stand. No one can stand alone, even think of it, without true *iman* in the heart.

With *iman* of the level Lut (PBUH) achieved, no job seems impossible. The rewards are worth the price. When unjust societies are overturned, the revolution usually starts with one person or one group willing to stand alone. They scorn the odds against them, because they believe in the Master of Odds and nothing else. All of Allah's prophets show that.

Lut's (PBUH) struggle teaches us we will be tested to prove how strong we really are. The test may be losing a job, losing a loved one, losing something material of high value, losing life. The immediate response is most important. Upon hearing distressing news, people often pray. What do they pray for? Do they seek Allah in patience or curse Him in frustration?

Life prepares us the way college students prepare for final exams. Students spend the semester in class attending lectures, reading material, taking tests and studying. Everything leads to one big final exam at the end of the course. The level of study, understanding and dedication students reach during the semester is directly related to their performance on the exam. Students who apply themselves diligently are confident going into the exam, while students who neglect their duty are nervous, hesitant, intimidated and frightened. Life works the same way.

> **(In falsehood will they be) until, when death comes to one of them, he says: "O my Lord send me back (to life) – in order that I may work righteousness in the things I neglected" – By no means! "It is but a word he says" – before them is a Partition till the Day they are raised up.**
>
> *Qur'an* 23:99-100

> **Such as took their religion to be mere amusement and play, and**

were deceived by the life of the world. That day shall We forget them as they forgot the meeting of this day of theirs, and as they were wont to reject Our Signs. For We had certainly sent unto them a Book based on knowledge, which We explained in detail - a guide and a mercy to all who believe.

Qur'an 7:51-52

The level of application and dedication we offer Allah prepares us for the final exam when we die. Unfortunately, some nations have to learn the hard way.

The Thamud tribe was blessed with power and glory throughout the land, but as with many nations, the more power they achieved, the more arrogant they became. They began to worship other gods beside Allah. One member of this community named Salih (PBUH) stood out as he was known for his wisdom and goodness. His people respected him until he advised them to check their attitude and behavior. They replied:

O Salih! Thou hast been one of us! A center of our hopes hitherto! Dost thou now forbid us the worship of what our fathers worshipped? But we are really in suspicious doubt as to that to which thou invitest us.

Qur'an 11:62

They knew he would not stop reproving them, so they gave him a task to keep him so busy he would eventually go away in shame: perform a miracle to prove you are telling the truth. They, however, wanted to choose the miracle, which was to make a unique she-camel appear from the mountains. Salih (PBUH) assembled the people together and took a vow from them that if he performed the miracle, they would stop worshiping other gods and worship Allah alone.

Salih (PBUH) prayed to Allah and ordered the people to look at the mountain. The she-camel appeared by Allah's permission, but He included a provision: leave the she-camel alone and let her roam freely. When the miracle happened, some of the people kept their word, but most did not. Those who reneged hated Salih (PBUH) and the she-camel. The rich among them plotted and finally killed the camel, for which the people praised them. Salih (PBUH) told them they had incurred Allah's wrath, at which they insolently asked that their punishment be hastened: **"O Salih! Bring about thy threats, if thou art a messenger of Allah!"** (*Qur'an* 7:77). They saw in Salih (PBUH) and his followers a sign of harm to come, so they plotted against him.

They said: "We consider you a bad omen you and those with you". He said: "Your ill omen is

with Allah, rather ye are a people under trial."

Qur'an 27:47

Nine men from the tribe planned to kill Salih (PBUH) one night, but destruction came upon them all before they could execute their plan. The most vehement in opposition were the wealthy, notables. That happens often in societies steeped in injustice. The wealthy know the oppressed want and deserve justice, yet the more wealth they receive the less they attribute their wealth to Allah. Allah rewards wealthy people who do not fall into that trap with even more wealth, as happened to Sulayman (PBUH).

The rich people who beset Salih (PBUH) felt that submission to The Message meant they would lose money, just as the tribes of Quraysh felt when Muhammad (PBUH) appeared.

Ignorance needs no clearer example. We often think all our benefits come from our own planning, but Salih's (PBUH) story shows that our plans are not sufficient to fulfill our desires. Societies that do not recognize that, limit their progress and destabilize themselves, requiring amending of laws constantly to accommodate their oligarchy but not to advance justice. Such societies have no problem giving tax breaks to the rich or cutting social programs designed to help the disadvantaged. If justice accords with the rule of Allah, however there is no need for amendments, since such a system guarantees the rights of all citizens, not just some.

The Thamud challenged Salih (PBUH) because they thought they could beat down his determination. They thought their numbers would give them an advantage, that they could intimidate him. Corrupt societies use the same technique. Both Salih (PBUH) and Lut (PBUH) confronted it.

The more things change, the more we must study the past and recall that we may struggle alone. At times the very people we try to help will abandon us and try to overwhelm us. That behavior pattern can come from anywhere, regardless of socioeconomic status.

Leaders must understand that reality. The people of Lut (PBUH) and Salih (PBUH) knew to follow their leader, but they refused—which saddened Lut (PBUH) and Salih (PBUH), but they had to move on. Both communities figured their prophets and leaders were responsible, not they themselves.

Today many communities have imams capable of developing strong communities to produce economic and political independence but are crippled by people unwilling to accept their own responsibility. It is not a question of worshiping other gods with Allah. There can be no more prophets or messengers after Muhammad (PBUH), so neither is the imams' authenticity the issue. Yet the unwillingness to commit to a goal that goes beyond private interest permeates like a cancer. Since chains are only as strong as their weakest link, communities are only as strong as their weakest members.

Selfish people know their communities' potential but prefer leisure to a difficult struggle that yields progress. They are quick to blame their leaders for *their* stagnation and shift the guilt away from themselves.

Lut (PBUH) and Salih (PBUH) could do no more than convey the message. Some communities today wrongly expect their leaders to do more than their share, displaying a lack of maturity and community concern. Some help their leaders only if there is something in it for them. Others notice that, and the community looks like a pool of leeches instead of an atmosphere of embracing the good and forbidding the wrong.

The communities of Lut (PBUH) and Salih (PBUH) knew both were of honorable and upright character. They had no reason to question the authenticity of what they were trying to do. Although communities may question their leaders to be sure they do not abuse their authority, some people question every goal their leaders want to accomplish, hoping all the while the leaders will require no assistance from them.

The strongest leaders cannot overcome such thinking. No matter if the community owns land for building schools, farms and businesses if no one is willing to teach, to till the land, to build the stores. If people cannot recognize or do not respect the kind of leadership described in the Qur'an, their imams' authority vanishes. Thus Allah's punishment was swift and relentless on the communities of Lut (PBUH) and Salih (PBUH).

Some people always wait to get involved until their leaders prove themselves. Like the community of Salih (PBUH), however, once the leader proves himself dedicated, people find other reasons to not get involved. That is why leaders are forced to search for assistants trained for community involvement, thus removing their focus away from community building. Useless people suck the life out of any growing community. Perhaps saddest is that such people are so self absorbed, they do not see their part in undoing the communities they claim to be so passionate about. Knowing that, Allah gave the communities of Lut (PBUH) and Salih (PBUH) years to come around. That is why strong communities today cannot be developed in a short time.

Contemporary communities assign different people different tasks, all associated *with* the community, but people must get involved and support their leaders. Leaders should not be left out in the cold when the struggle intensifies, but rather supported when they are right and checked when they are wrong. Lut (PBUH) and Salih (PBUH) never got the chance for that. Their communities prevented it!

Leaders must recognize enemies from all walks of life, internal and external. Up to this point, I have focused on the external, but internal enemies are equally lethal because they say they want to help reach the community's goals but in fact do everything to frustrate them. External enemies are open and honest from the beginning, and leaders can clearly spot the traps they lay for the community. Successful leaders must overcome both.

Leaders must be able to stand alone, since they never know when the people will desert them. They must always have contingency plans. Lut (PBUH) and Salih (PBUH) never overcame their internal enemies. Leaders must keep that possibility in their mind to avoid becoming depressed when the community attitude turns negative. Lut (PBUH) and Salih (PBUH) endured constant stress with no one to confide in, no one to help. They had to repeatedly invite people they knew would show them no respect. Non-prophetic leaders would have buckled under the stress, frustration and strain. Long before hypertension was diagnosed, Lut (PBUH) and Salih (PBUH) knew all about it—and worse.

The prophets and messengers were the best of humanity because they never lost their drive or dedication. They were the paragons of the servants of Allah! Good leaders today hope to follow in their footsteps, and communities should support them.

> Say ye: "We believe in Allah and the revelation given to us, and to Ibrahim, Ismail, Ishaq, Yaqub, and the tribes, and that given to Musa and Isa, and that given to all prophets from their Lord: We make no distinction between one and another of them: :and we bow to Allah (in Islam)"
>
> *Qur'an* 2:136

Standing alone is vital to any leader and essential to understanding a community. It is not a characteristic we can turn on or off, since the iman in our hearts produces it. With no iman, we cannot stand alone, as history and the Qur'an teach us. We must take heed or risk failure. Once this stand has been determined, a place of community organization must be established to permanently ground the stand.

VALUE
OF
THE
MASJID

Several aspects must be recalled when establishing a community based *masjid*. What is its purpose? What issues affect the people who live around it? How will the *masjid* help resolve them? Today few Muslims can answer those questions because they do not consider them in the light of Qur'an and the example of Muhammad (PBUH). Several ingredients must be consistent for a *masjid* to grow and thrive: purpose, brotherhood, leadership and community support.

> **And those who built a masjid or hurt [the Muslims], to spread unbelief, to disunite [the believers] and to await him who had fought Allah and His Messenger, they will certainly swear that they meant nothing but good. Allah bears witness that they are liars. Do not stand up there [for prayer] for a masjid founded on piety from the first day is worthier of your standing in it. Therein are men who love to be purified; and Allah loves those who purify themselves.**
>
> *Qur'an* 9:107-108

Allah explains that just as the enemies of Al-Islam unite to destroy the message, just as they use symbols (in this case a *masjid*) to confuse Muslims, truly committed individuals must establish their *masjid* to unite everyone who wants to obey Allah and His Messenger (PBUH) in order to offset and resist attacks on

Al-Islam. In many cities throughout the USA, Muslims have at times turned the House of Allah into a cultural center, a kind of country club. In Muhammad's (PBUH) day, obedience to Allah and faithfulness to the example of His Messenger (PBUH) determined believers' worth, not their social or professional status.

A *masjid* should originate and operate under the guidance of the Qur'an and *Sunnah*. Decisions affecting Muslims and neighboring non-Muslim communities should be made through *Shura* (mutual consultation), not by a board of directors. Allah insists that worshippers stick to these principles to gain His support and strength in the many struggles of life.

Muslims must control every facet concerning the application of Al-Islam. *Whatever one doesn't control can and will be used against them by their enemy.* Muhammad (PBUH) established a school after he set up the *masjid* in Medina, because he knew that if Muslims do not educate their children about the love of Allah, the friends of Shaytan would educate them about everything *except* Allah.

Collective education requires collective brotherhood, so Muhammad (PBUH) instituted *muakhat* (the process of making brothers). In Arabia then, tribal warfare was as commonplace as street gang violence today. The most pervasive gang wars then were between one group called *Aus* and another called *Khazraj*. Once they accepted the message of Al-Islam, they practiced *muakhat* to prevent the return of strife.

Muhammad (PBUH) explained that the *Aus* and the *Khazraj* were brothers because their belief in Allah united them. Once they understood that, men once bitter enemies locked in intertribal warfare renounced violence. The rich gave half their wealth to others in the spirit of true brotherhood. In addition, they rechanneled their energy from fighting each other to fighting Allah's enemies and they became known as *Ansars* (helpers in the cause of Allah). They finally realized that they could not help Allah's Message shine if they did not overcome tribal divisions: **"Allah will never change the condition of a people until they change the condition within themselves"** *(Qur'an* 13:11).

When true brotherhood is practiced, no Muslim can fail to feel another's pain, though they may not physically suffer. True brotherhood does not let one neglect another in need, since the entire community would pay a heavy price.

Muhammad's (PBUH) companion Ibn Abbas was in a state of *itikaf* (retreating to the *masjid* for extended periods of worship) when a sad looking man sat down next to him. Ibn Abbas asked if anything was wrong, and the man said he could not pay a debt he owed. Ibn Abbas offered to speak to the creditor on his companion's behalf. The man replied with amazement, "Have you forgotten that you were in a state of *itikaf?*" Ibn Abbas reminded him that Prophet Muhammad (PBUH) said that to help a neighbor is better than doing *itikaf* for ten years; and anyone who performs *itikaf* for one day seeking the pleasure of Allah creates a distance of three ditches between himself and hellfire, each ditch as wide as the abyss between east and west or between Heaven and earth.

Ibn Abbas could have ignored his brother's problems since he was not directly affected and stayed in *itikaf.* He knew, however, of Allah's blessings when concern is shown for those in need. Too many Muslims choose not to get involved in each other's affairs, because they see no personal loss for themselves. That reveals a lack of brotherhood. If we practiced true brotherhood today, the kind Muhammad's (PBUH) companions learned, famine victims in Niger would get immense assistance from so-called Muslim countries around the world. Political prisoners like Imam Jamil Al Amin would be center stage at mass Muslim gatherings such as *Eid* (two festivals that celebrate the end of Ramadan and the Day of Sacrifice) instead of politicians who want a vote from communities they don't respect. Yet many Muslims hardly notice these things, because we are detached from true *muakhat.*

Once the *masjid's* purpose is established and everyone is united in brotherhood to fulfill that purpose, someone must determine the best way to use the Qur'an and *Sunnah* to establish Allah's way, to ensure the rights of people and the oppressed, to embrace the right and forbid the wrong. What issues affect the *masjid's* community most? How will the community's purpose and the unity of brotherhood be used to solve them? Providing answers and deriving solutions to these concerns is the task of true leadership. That is the imam's job.

Allah gave us everything we need to survive and excel, and we must learn how to combine one part with the other. Three elements are needed to create fire— oxygen, fuel and a spark. Without these elements combined, no fire, and man would never have learned to cook food, generate heat, or light his dwelling. The community *masjid* uses the same formula.

As the *masjid* may grow and survive, people must be willing to work in the cause of Allah for the pleasure of Allah (oxygen). They must feed on the guidance of the Qur'an and Muhammad's (PBUH) *Sunnah* as fuel, and the imam combines the two in the right proportions as a spark. If one of the ingredients lacks, the *masjid* will not survive. If all ingredients are present, no matter if the building is worth five million or five thousand, it will become and remain a beacon of light emitting powerful heat in a city of cold hearted darkness!

Many Muslims err in thinking that imams must sustain *masjids* by themselves; if something goes wrong, they alone are to blame. Such thinking left *Bani Israel* (Children of Israel) wandering in the wilderness forty years. They expected Musa (PBUH) and Allah alone to fight the army that occupied the promised land Allah guaranteed would be theirs—though only if they were collectively willing to fight for it. As a result, the weak among them died in the wilderness, and the strong had to wait forty years to enter the land.

Even though imams are leaders, if communities do not unite in brotherhood and work and sacrifice for Allah, everyone suffers. In spite of Musa's (PBUH) knowledge and commitment to the struggle, this was one lesson not even he could teach *Bani Israel*. Once a fire is lit, the spark is no longer needed. If the fuel and oxygen are pure, the imam can be replaced, and the *masjid* should continue to grow. If the people are niggardly and selfish or like *Bani Israel* don't want to obey the commands of the Qur'an and *Sunnah*, the result is catastrophic failure. The imam can only spark the blaze; everyone else must help sustain the fire.

> **And whether We show you a part of what We promise them or cause you to die, your duty is to deliver the Message and it is for Us to do the reckoning.**
>
> *Qur'an* 13:40

In addition to qualities already discussed, the imam must have the following characteristics.

1) He must be committed to work and sacrifice

for the cause of Allah more than anyone else in the community. He must take the initiative to learn what he does not know. He should have such *taqwa* (fear of Allah) that he is ready to say, "I don't know the answer to the question. Let me research it and get back to you," or simply "Allah knows best" about matters unknown to him.

He must not seek leadership to gratify his own ego but rather must understand that he holds the post to serve people, not vice versa. That is why Muhammad (PBUH) said, "If anyone desires leadership, he should not have it." The person with the most *taqwa* knows he will be held accountable to Allah on the Day of Judgment for everything that goes on in his community and does not want that burden: **"The Day will come when We will call every people with their leader."** (*Qur'an* 17:71).

Therefore those with leadership fear Allah too much to manipulate the position. Allah will bless them with the capacity to grow in knowledge and stature in ways beneficial to the community of the *masjid* and Al-Islam as a whole: **"O you who believe, if you support Allah, He will support you and steady your footsteps"** (*Qur'an* 47:7).

2) Leaders must understand and accept that most in the community will rarely appreciate their effort and sacrifice. For the most part they will receive no thanks or acknowledgment. If someone complains, the

imam must listen and take it to heart. They must understand that Allah alone rewards them and must be their sole source of motivation.

> **If you turn away, I have asked for no reward from you. My reward is only with Allah. I have been ordered to be one of those who submit.**
>
> *Qur'an* 10:72

He will hear encouragement rarely but complaints and criticism often.

> **But the Messenger and those who believe with him struggle with their wealth and their lives. To those are the good things reserved, and those are the prosperous. Allah has prepared for them Gardens beneath which rivers flow, abiding therein forever. That is the great triumph!**
>
> *Qur'an* 9:88-89

Because imams alone endure at that particular level, many times they feel alone.

3) Leaders must have *tawakkul,* trust and confidence that Allah will see them through difficulties and help them overcome them.

> **O ye who believe! Call in remembrance the favor of Allah unto you when certain men formed the design to stretch out their hands against you, but (Allah) held back their hands from you: so fear Allah. And on Allah let believers put (all) their trust.**

> *Qur'an* 5:11

4) They must love and work for Allah even in the face of personal hardship. Grief often saddens people in the community, and they rely on the imam to boost their spirits with a good spiritual lesson. If the imam despairs, people focus on that instead of the message.

5) They must identify key people with expertise in various areas who can get things done if other matters occupy the imam. Imams cannot know everything. They must be patient with the community and give them time to develop and improve, since they may not share the imam's level of commitment. The community in turn must provide good counsel to assist the

imam to make good decisions through *Shura.*

It was by a mercy from Allah that you dealt leniently with them for had you been cruel and hard hearted, they would have abandoned you. So pardon them, ask Allah's Forgiveness for them, and consult them in the conduct of affairs. Then when you are resolved, trust in Allah; Allah indeed loves those who trust in Him.

Qur'an 3:159

The imam's position is not to be envied. These qualities do not guarantee a successful *masjid.* Its members *must* support the imam and the *masjid.* The experience of *Bani Israel* shows the necessity of community support of its leaders. The community must care enough about the *masjid* not only to give the imam advice but also to participate in making that advice effective. Muslims must be willing to work in and around the *masjid.* They must be willing to support it financially as well.

Only those who believe in Allah and the Hereafter, performs the prayers, gives the alms and fears no one but Allah, shall visit [and maintain] Allah's masjids. Those shall be reckoned among the rightly

guided."

Qur'an 9:18

Allah created everything to have balance, especially community based masjids.

> **And thus have We made you a balanced community, so that you may bear witness unto the rest of mankind, and that the Messenger may bear witness unto you.**
>
> *Qur'an* 2:143

All have a role to play. When brotherhood fails or Muslims refuse to give their support, all responsibility falls on the imam, creating an imbalance which can keep the light of Al-Islam from those who need it most. Muslims must be engaged in *Shura* because the imam will need assistance. That is an excellent way of letting imams know what specific talent is available to them and what resources the community based *masjid* has.

Without interior resources, imams must look outside the community, which also disturbs the balance. Without help from within, imams must make decisions without hearing all sides and may unintentionally make a bad judgment, which the slackers are quick to complain about. Muslims who do not understand that fail to see how their lack of involvement fosters bad results. The community should not ask anything of the imam they are not willing to help with.

> **Those of the believers who
> sit at home while suffering from no
> injury are not equal to those who
> fight [and struggle] for the cause of
> Allah with their possessions and per-
> sons. Allah has raised those who
> fight [and struggle] with possessions
> and persons one degree over those
> who stay at home; and to each Allah
> has promised the fairest good. Yet
> Allah has granted a great reward to
> those who fight and not to those who
> stay behind.**
>
> *Qur'an* 4:95

People complain if imams in the ghetto do not give the same *khutbas* (formal religious talks) and lessons as imams in the suburbs. Yet, **"We have sent forth no Messenger except in the tongue of his own people so that he may expound to them clearly"** (*Qur'an* 14:4).

People often fail to realize that each community has different needs, and imams must diagnose what the communities they serve need. The ghetto and suburban socioeconomic structures produce different problems for the people in them. Thus the message of Al-Islam remains the same but is communicated in diverse ways. The community owes the imam that understanding and the benefit of the doubt. Those who support the *masjid* will try to understand the imams. They will not hesitate to approach them and try to understand their goals and ideas. Those who don't care and are around only when it suits their interest desert the *masjid* without consulting the imam as their inability to understand problems in their entirety arrests their vision.

Whenever someone died in Medina, Muhammad (PBUH) always went to wash and bury the body and pray for the soul. That taxed his time, since he had other matters to deal with, like marital counseling, family issues, leading prayers, teaching the Qur'an, *etc.* In spite of that he never complained. Once the community noticed that, however, they decided to bring the dead to Muhammad (PBUH) to relieve him of the journey and help him handle other affairs as well. The community should offer the imam such understanding and support. It is the epitome of the *Ansar* (the helpers in Allah's Cause). His people's support was so great it prompted Muhammad (PBUH) to say, "If one group of people went in one direction, and the Ansars went into a ravine, I would follow the Ansars."

Purpose, brotherhood, leadership and support are essential to creating, establishing, maintaining, and growing a community based *masjid*. We should not devalue that way of life to gain favor with its enemies. As Allah has said, **"Today, I have perfected My Grace on you and approved Islam as your complete way of life"** (*Qur'an* 5:3).

We must neglect nothing in the Qur'an or *Sunnah* to please others. No other –ism, be it capitalism, modernism, or secularism, is required, because Al-Islam is already perfect and complete, its standard of purpose outlined in the Book of Allah, its standard of brotherhood exemplified by the *Aus* and *Khazraj*, its standard of leadership Muhammad's (PBUH), its standard of community support given by the *Ansars*. These virtues influence the true value of any *masjid*.

VALUE OF THE STRUGGLE OF THE AFRICAN AMERICAN

We have certainly created man to toil and struggle.

Qur'an 90:4

To succeed, we must first understand that struggle is the natural state for all human beings—because Allah says so. Yet we must ask, "Why would Allah say that?" Allah created mankind to need Him for everything related to our survival. Since Allah only is truly independent and without need, all humans should recognize that they need Allah more than Allah needs them.

Mankind has free will within the context of Allah's power. Allah lets us struggle for everything in this life, so we guard and protect what we have. If we did not have to struggle, ease of accomplishment might dull our appreciation. We would become arrogant, haughty and prideful.

By requiring us to struggle, Allah gives us each the opportunity to recall His role in everything. By asking us to struggle, Allah lets us understand that anyone can use His gifts to overcome. We must embrace struggle, for it is inevitable. Once we accept struggle, we must identify and study its phases.

Allah expects us to overcome anything that calls us to worship all except Him. Our ultimate goal is to understand that and rise above such things to become leaders charged with helping people worship Allah: "**It** is He Who hath made you His agents, inheritors of the earth" (*Qur'an* 6:165).

In this book, I have addressed qualities and characteristics from which all people, Muslim and non-Muslim, can benefit. I have shown the care and compassionate attention Allah reserves for the oppressed, and I would be remiss not to address a group of people whose history of oppression is unique: the African-Americans. The distinctly horrible history of the transatlantic slave trade laid the foundation of America's economy as it strove to establish its independence from Britain. Since then African Americans have been the first victims to feel the full weight of racism.

> **O mankind, indeed, We have created you from male and female and made you into different nations and tribes so that you may know one another.**
>
> *Qur'an* 49:13

In this verse, Allah made racism unlawful. As it is wrong to hate people for the color of their skin, so it is wrong to hate *yourself* because of skin color or any other physical characteristic.

When people learn to hate themselves, no external force is needed to oppress them. When people are taught to hate themselves, oppression is internalized and automatic. The American slave owners knew that if they pitted male against female, the light skinned against the dark, and preferred one over the other, the slaves would develop self-hatred and pass it from generation to generation. Several American laws and behavior rooted in racism fostered a group inferiority complex among many African-Americans. African-Americans cannily perceived that the key to survival was to make their oppressors comfortable with their superiority complex. Light-skinned Blacks were sometimes able to pass for White. Blacks with thick lips and broad noses were assured they were the worst of the worst, absolutely worthless.

Some tried to straighten or bleach their hair, hoping that if they looked White they might be treated White. Such behavior resulted from the psychological and ideological warfare designed to perpetuate the oppression. Blacks sought ways to find a culture and an identity (since both had been stolen) to restore and uplift their spirits. Many found what they *thought* was Al-Islam.

The ideology of white supremacy taught that White people were the standard of every excellence. Likewise, Muslims who came from other countries had their own superiority complex. Blacks in America who turned to them for Islamic understanding heard instead that everything Islamic was defined by cultures that had nothing to do with Al-Islam but everything to do with an ethnicity not theirs.

Some African-Americans then felt inferior not only because they weren't White but also because they were not part of another country's Muslim cultures. In a way, some African-Americans became colonized a second time. Today some Muslim African-Americans change their dialect to give others the impression they hail from overseas. Some Muslim African-Americans think they must dress in a particular way that disguises them as something other than what Allah made them.

Some Muslim African-Americans even say, "I'm not African American, I'm just Muslim." If they truly valued the racial makeup Allah blessed them with, they would not do everything possible to hide it. One rarely meets a Muslim from Egypt or Pakistan who denies he is Egyptian or Pakistani. Consequently, many non-Muslim African-Americans who consider themselves Pan-Africanists, and Black nationalists want nothing to do with being Muslim. This occurs, because the African American has been conditioned to think neither he nor his legacy has any value. However, nothing could be more contrary.

There would be no CAIR (Council of American Islamic Relations) had there had been no NAACP (National Association for the Advancement of Colored People). There would be no ISNA (Islamic Society of North America) without a SNCC (Student Non-Violent Coordinating Committee). Many movements from countries outside America that claim to spread proper Islam would not have grown as they have without the rank and file Muslim African-Americans who initially energized them. Long before the multi-million dollar suburban *masjids* in White suburbia were built, tiny humble *masjids* held together with tape and glue were operating in the ghettos.

The Black liberation struggle enabled people from other countries to take advantage of affirmative action and build homes in former racially restricted areas. Everyone but the African-American fully understands this and has been able to capitalize on that value. The day the African American completely realizes their worth will be the day social, political, educational and economic independence become possible. Those who benefit from this oppression, however, quote *Qur'an* 49:13 (see above) to convince African-Americans their racial background offers nothing of value but the legacy of enslavement. That is to misconstrue the verse.

Allah revealed the verse because He knew that *all* racial groups would have historical highs and lows. The way each deals with its success or hardship is directly related to its specific identity. In other words, we should appreciate the different gifts and talents Asians bring. We should appreciate the gifts and talents of Africans. We should appreciate the gifts and talents of Europeans, of Mexicans, Puerto Ricans, Cubans and all others, too numerous to name.

Allah does not intend one race to reign over any other, so He gave each unique qualities which combined, can create a powerful interdependent alliance to produce more dedication and commitment to Allah's worship.

For any group to deny another's value, is to say that the blessings Allah gives us all are a curse for some! That is why He **"created us into different nations and tribes so that we may know one another."** When people are stripped of their value—as Black people, the only immigrants forced to come to America, robbed of their family names, languages, cultures and religions—they are lost. The people who capitalized on all that and do so yet need to seek Allah's forgiveness and the forgiveness of those from whose oppression they profit.

A people's experience gives them a sense of their roots, helps them appreciate what they have, motivates them to protect and preserve it. That is how we come to know and respect one another. No one should apologize for the features Allah gave him. Those who denied their uniqueness should apologize. Know your value, learn your worth and let not one who does not respect you or your legacy set your socioeconomic, political or spiritual agenda. Be the leader within you.

Among Al-Islam's goals is to create and maintain a constant state of awareness, which leads to the proper consciousness. I have examined a few characteristics that can be useful in one's struggle toward an increased human worth. Before Muhammad (PBUH) undertook the mission of being the final prophet, the society of which he was part practiced female infanticide, gang warfare, sexual license and other immoralities, a society as backward as many who today are called worthless. Still, Allah blessed it and changed it with Al-Islam. Those whom society calls worthless, Allah treasures.

He who has in his heart the weight of a mustard seed of pride shall not enter Paradise.
Verily, Allah is Graceful and He loves Grace.
Pride is disdaining the truth (out of self-conceit) and showing contempt for a people.
Prophet Muhammad (PBUH)

A man asked Prophet Muhammad (PBUH), "Is it wrong or a part of prejudice that a man should love his tribal people?"

The Prophet (PBUH) responded, "No, what is wrong is when this man
supports his tribal people when they are committing oppression."
Source - *Ibn Majah - The Book of Turmoils*

ISLAMandRACE.COM

The need for addressing the many issues raised in this book make necessary a dedicated website, designed to forge an international movement to work toward improving the social, political and economic conditions of one's own community first and all else after.

IslamAndRace.com (I&R) is the brainchild of author Amir Makin featuring Muslim news, Black news, politics, issues of racism and Islam in the Quran. It provides a point of view never sought when discussions arise.

The Muslim African American is routinely ignored and discounted even though a 2007 Pew Study of all American born Muslims that choose to practice Al Islam stated nearly 60% are African American. It is increasingly clear this voice must be heard to prevent further misrepresentations arising from this important vantage point.

IslamAndRace.com provides in depth analysis

on politics,Islam and racism. Black news and Muslim news will be presented. For understanding Islam on these issues there is also understanding from the Quran. We will offer products and services designed to champion causes of justice that go unheard of in the corporate controlled media. We are 100% independently owned. We pride ourselves in reporting on events that some choose to ignore, including those in the Islamic community and outside of it.

IslamAndRace.com will cover Muslm news and Black news on a global level with particular focus on the impact that race, religion and politics have. I&R will use its voice to deconstruct, educate and plainly state a very different perspective.

Six Point Platform

1. **End mandatory minimum sentencing** as it has caused people of all colors to be jailed without due process. The application of mandatory minimums have given prosecutors the power to selectively charge people with crimes carrying the harshest of sentences for

minor offenses which should be reserved for the worst of offenders. A 2011 Congressional United States Sentencing Commission report for Black news stated, "Black offenders were subject to the mandatory minimum penalty . . . 60.6 percent of their offenses carrying such a penalty, followed by Hispanic (41.0%) and White (36.3%) offenders."

2. **End the war on drugs** as it has been used as a pretext to justify racial profiling on Black people primarily. All federal funds used in this endeavor should be redirected toward the creation of youth vocational after school activities, neighborhood development projects, in conjunction with substance abuse rehabilitation and mental health programs.

3. **End all racial profiling** in law enforcement as it has resulted in too many false arrests, imprisonment, exonerations and deaths of mostly African Americans, Latinos and some poor Caucasians for crimes they never committed. This has given rise to the current stop and frisk program openly practiced by the NYPD, spying on Muslims as admitted by

the NJ attorney general, and several more in-
dignities. Federal law should classify these acts
as criminal offenses, rather than a civil act vio-
lation. Federal funding should be withheld
from those agencies shown to regularly engage in this practice.

4. **End all military conflicts and wars for profit** (the control of another nation's natural resources to include oil, gold, diamonds, and natural metals). Both democratic and republican parties have supported wars for oil (Iraq, Afghanistan, Somalia) instead of spending the monies for war on empowering those beset by poverty and disenfranchisement in America.

5. **Provide immediate tax reliefs to independently funded educational programs and homeschooling parents** so the income they are forced to forego in paying tax dollars into a public education system which often ill prepares Black children for future success. It also restricts access to college prepatory and entrepreneurship based curriculums.

6. **Create an international campaign to identify, address, and account for the**

events caused through centuries of institutional white supremacy and racism. The greatest social problem in America has been institutional white supremacy and racism as it has played a role in everything from the structuring of neighborhoods, electoral politics, to the implementation of state and federal laws. Its effects should no longer be ignored. The American society must commit itself to understanding the origins of this problem, and work tirelessly in all attempts to confront it with the same veracity demonstrated in movements to acheive cancer awareness.

LEXICON

AH – stands for **a**fter the **h**ijra which marks the time that Prophet Muhammad (PBUH) was forced to leave the town of Mecca as it had become physically hostile for himself and the Muslims so they could flee to the safe and secure town of Medina

ALLAH - the Lord of All, The Creator of all things who has never manifested Himself on Earth. This is Arabic which means the All Knowing All Powerful God in English: He has no partners or associates, no sons or daughters and is above all forms of human representation

AMIR – one who is appointed as a leader by the Caliph and placed in charge of accomplishing one task or a specific group of tasks

ASR – the afternoon prayer

CALIPH – leader of a Muslim statehood

CALIPHATE – one's tenure of being a caliph

CE - Christian Era

DEEN – way of life known as Al-Islam

DHUR – the noon prayer

FAJR – the morning prayer

HAJJ – the trip one must take at least once in a life-time to the Ka'bah built in Mecca by Prophet Ibrahim (PBUH) and his son Ismail

HIJRA – leaving one country that has become unsafe for Muslims to live in for a country that offers peace and security
ILM - Knowledge

IMAM – leader of community prayers; leader of a masjid and all other religious duties

IMAN – faith

ITIKAF – process of retreating to the masjid for extended periods of worship

ISHA – the late evening prayer

JINN – beings created from fire that have free will to choose to worship Allah or follow Satan

KA'BAH – first masjid built for the purpose of praying to Allah which was constructed at the Divine Instruction of Allah

LA ILLAHA ILL ALLAH – there is no god worthy

of worship but **GOD**

MAGHRIB – the sunset prayer

MUAKHAT – the process of making brothers

MUSLIM – one who voluntarily submits their will to the will and commands of Allah by obeying His Laws and Orders

PBUH – peace be upon him

RAMADAN – the month of obligatory fasting; 9th month on the Muslim calendar

SABR – patience

SALAT – the officially prescribed prayer of the Muslim for a minimum of 5 obligatory daily prayers; always consist of different bodily positions in order to synchronize one's heart, and tongue with ones actions to represent the highest form of worship
SHAYTAN – Arabic for Satan

SUNNAH – The life example and implementation of the Qur'an that Prophet Muhammad (PBUH) and all other prophets that came before him put into daily practice

TAQWA – fear of Allah

TAWAKKUL – total trust in Allah

ZAKAT – obligatory charity one must give as 2.5% of one's wealth

BIBLIOGRAPHY

Al Amin, Jamil Imam. *Revolution By The Book: The Rap Is Live.* Writer's International, 1993.

Ali, Abdullah Yusuf. *The Meaning of The Holy Qur'an.* Amana Publications, 2004.

Al-Mubarakpuri, Sheikh Safiur-Rahman. *Tafsir Ibn Kathir.* Dar-Us-Salam Publications, 2000.

Bukhari, Muhammad ibn Ismail. *Sahih Bukhari.* Al Saadawi Publications, 1996.

Churchill, Ward and Jim Vander Wall. *Cointelpro Papers: Documents from the FBI's Secret Wars Against Domestic Dissent.* South End, 1991.

Dan Fodio, Sheikh Uthman. *Handbook on Islam.* Madinah Press, 1996.

Diouf, Sylvianne. *Servants of Allah: African Muslims Enslaved in the Americas.* New York University Press, 1998.

El Hajj Malik El Shabazz, Malcolm. *The Autobiography of Malcolm X: As Told to Alex Haley.* Ballantine Books, 1987.

Ezzedin, Ibrahim and Denys Johnson Davies. *Forty Hadith Qudsi*. Islamic Texts Society, 1997.

Khan, Majid and Maulana Muhammad Yusuf Kandlawi. *Hayatus Sahabah: The Lives of Sahabah*. Ahmad Printing Corporation, 1999.

Malik, Imam. *Muwatta of Imam Malik*. Kitab Bhavan, 1996.

Muslim bin Hajaj bin Naysaburi, Imam. *Sahih Muslim*. Dar Al Kotob & Jarir Bookstore, 2005.

Reiman, Jeffrey. *The Rich Get Richer and the Poor Get Prison 6th Edition*. Allyn & Bacon. 2000.

Millionaire Durst Acquitted of Neighbor's Murder. 11 Nov. 2003. Cable News Network. 11 Nov. 2003 <http://www.cnn.com/2003/LAW/11/11/ctv.durst>

The Exoneree. 14-20 Sep. 2006. Philadelphia City Paper. 14-20 Sep. 2006 <http://www.citypaper.net/articles/2006-09-14/cb.shtml>

The Story of Harold Wilson: Convicted of Triple Murder, Sentenced to Die, Exonerated after 17 Years in Prison. 20 Dec. 2005. Democracy Now!. 20 Dec. 2005 <http://www.democracynow.org/article.pl?sid=05/12/20/1434244>

Al Amin, Karima. *The Case of Imam Jamil Abdullah Al Amin.* 2006. <http://www.mana-net.org/pages.php?ID=activism&ID2=&NUM=46>

Imam Jamil Al Amin at Florence Colo., Supermax. 19 Sep. 2007. San Francisco Bay View. 19 Sep. 2007. <http://www.sfbayview.com/20070919430/News/Behind_Enemy_Lines/Imam_Jamil_Al-Amin_at_Florence_Colo._Supermax.html>

Atlanta area officer dies after shootout. 17 Mar. 2000. CNN. 17 Mar. 2000.<http://archives.cnn.com/2000/US/03/17/officers.shot.03/>

A.I.C Publications Order Form

Please send me:

_______ of copies of *A Worthy Muslim: Quranic Tools Needed to Overcome Oppression and Imperialism In Order to Institute Justice*

At a price of ($12.95 each + $3.99 Shipping) = $16.94 for 1 book plus($12.95 + $1.50 shipping) or $14.45 for each additional book.

Total Amount enclosed: _____________________

To: _________________________________

____

____

Send form along with check or money order to:

A.I.C Publications
PO Box 181467
Arlington, TX 76002-1467
submissions@AICPublications.com

Please allow 2-3 weeks for delivery.